AI-driven Strategic Management: Navigating the Future of Business

Authored by

Esther Asiedu

Department of Management Studies
Business School Ghana Communication
Technology University, Tesano-Accra
Ghana

AI-driven Strategic Management: Navigating the Future of Business

Author: Esther Asiedu

ISBN (Online): 979-8-89881-144-0

ISBN (Print): 979-8-89881-145-7

ISBN (Paperback): 979-8-89881-146-4

Published by Bentham Science Publishers Pte. Ltd. Singapore, in collaboration with Eureka Conferences, USA. All Rights Reserved.

First published in 2025.

need for a court order if at any point you breach any terms of this License Agreement. In no event will any delay or failure by Bentham Science Publishers in enforcing your compliance with this License Agreement constitute a waiver of any of its rights.

3. You acknowledge that you have read this License Agreement, and agree to be bound by its terms and conditions. To the extent that any other terms and conditions presented on any website of Bentham Science Publishers conflict with, or are inconsistent with, the terms and conditions set out in this License Agreement, you acknowledge that the terms and conditions set out in this License Agreement shall prevail.

Bentham Science Publishers Pte. Ltd.
No. 9 Raffles Place
Office No. 26-01
Singapore 048619
Singapore
Email: subscriptions@benthamscience.net

**BENTHAM
SCIENCE**

CONTENTS

FOREWORD

As a business leader who has spent decades navigating the ever-changing landscape of corporate strategy, I have seen technological innovations come and go. However, few developments have had as profound an impact As artificial Intelligence. The dawn of AI represents not just an evolution but a revolution in how businesses make decisions, allocate resources, and engage with customers.

This book, AI-driven Strategic Management: Navigating the Future of Business, is both timely and necessary. The author has done an exceptional job of exploring the vast potential AI holds for strategic management while addressing the complexities and challenges it introduces. As we stand on the brink of this new era, it is crucial for business leaders, entrepreneurs, and strategists to understand how AI can be integrated into their strategic vision.

I have had the privilege of working with organizations that are leading the way in AI adoption. The results are undeniable: improved decision-making, greater efficiency, and the ability to foresee and adapt to market shifts more rapidly than ever before. However, with great power comes great responsibility. The ethical implications of AI and its potential to disrupt industries cannot be ignored.

The book offers not only a roadmap for navigating the future of AI in business but also an invitation to engage thoughtfully with this transformative technology. I highly recommend this book to anyone seeking to understand how AI is reshaping the world of strategic management.

Mohammed Majeed
Department of Marketing
Tamale Technical University
Ghana

PREFACE

In recent years, AI has moved from being a futuristic concept to a fundamental driver of business transformation. When I first began researching the intersection of AI and strategic management, it became clear that we are witnessing a paradigm shift in how businesses approach strategy. The ability to process and analyze data at scale, automate decision-making processes, and anticipate market changes in real-time is giving businesses an unprecedented level of agility and foresight.

This book is the culmination of years of research, analysis, and conversations with thought leaders and practitioners in the fields of AI and business strategy. I have witnessed firsthand the profound changes that AI has brought to organizations across various sectors, from finance and healthcare to manufacturing and retail. However, there is still a gap in understanding how to fully integrate AI into strategic management frameworks. Many organizations are either hesitant to adopt AI due to fear of the unknown, or they have implemented AI solutions without a cohesive strategy to guide their usage.

AI-driven Strategic Management: Navigating the Future of Business aims to bridge this gap by offering both theoretical insights and practical approaches. My hope is that this book will empower business leaders to confidently embrace AI as a powerful tool for innovation, optimization, and long-term success.

Esther Asiedu
Department of Management Studies
Business School Ghana Communication
Technology University, Tesano-Accra
Ghana

INTRODUCTION

The rapid advancement of Artificial Intelligence (AI) has transformed industries across the globe, revolutionizing the way businesses operate, compete, and innovate. In the realm of strategic management, AI is no longer a distant concept or experimental tool; it is a game-changer that is reshaping decision-making processes, market strategies, and organizational structures. AI-driven tools now enable businesses to analyze vast amounts of data, forecast market trends with unprecedented accuracy, and automate complex tasks, allowing leaders to focus on innovation and value creation.

This book, AI-driven Strategic Management: Navigating the Future of Business, probes into how AI is revolutionizing the core aspects of business strategy. From harnessing the power of predictive analytics to optimizing resource allocation, AI has become an essential component in developing competitive advantages in the modern business landscape. As organizations face an increasingly complex and dynamic environment, AI provides the insights and capabilities to navigate uncertainty, optimize operations, and foster sustainable growth.

Throughout this book, we explore practical applications, ethical considerations, and challenges associated with integrating AI into strategic management. Whether you are a business leader, entrepreneur, or strategist, this book will provide valuable insights and actionable strategies to leverage AI in shaping the future of your organization.

CHAPTER 1

An Overview of the Revolution of Artificial Intelligence (AI) in Strategic Management

Abstract: This chapter explores the transformative role of Artificial Intelligence (AI) in strategic management, focusing on its impact on organizational functions, data analysis, and executive decision-making. The research highlights that AI is no longer an optional tool but a necessity for strategic planning, project management, and organizational alignment. Companies that successfully integrate AI into their management practices benefit from enhanced efficiency, real-time data-driven decision-making, and improved adaptability to market changes. AI-powered solutions provide a competitive advantage by enabling businesses to streamline operations, enhance predictive capabilities, and optimize resource allocation. Organizations should proactively invest in AI technologies to strengthen their strategic management practices. Business leaders must foster a synergy between human expertise and AI-driven insights to maximize the benefits of AI integration. Continuous refinement of AI systems and alignment with organizational goals will be critical for long-term success. Businesses that embrace AI's full potential will remain competitive and innovative in an evolving corporate landscape.

Keywords: AI, Companies, Decision making, Management, Strategic, Strategy development, Strategy execution, Strategy evaluation.

INTRODUCTION

In the current fast-paced market, successful strategic management is crucial for businesses of all sizes. As industries rapidly transform, companies that do not swiftly adjust risk falling behind, becoming obsolete, or even ceasing to exist. The repercussions of inadequate strategic management are severe, including lost opportunities, reduced market share, and an inability to handle unexpected challenges. To circumvent these issues, progressive organizations are overhauling their strategy development methods. Traditional, slow approaches are being replaced by more flexible, responsive techniques that allow businesses to remain relevant in swiftly changing environments. This transition indicates a growing understanding that strategy must evolve from a yearly, static exercise to a continuous and dynamic process. In this pursuit of strategic flexibility, Artificial Intelligence (AI) has emerged as a revolutionary tool. AI enables businesses to outperform competitors by delivering swift, precise, and instantaneous insights. By leveraging AI, companies can analyze enormous datasets, recognize emerging patterns, and make well-informed decisions with unparalleled speed and accuracy. This technological advantage allows organizations to not only keep up with change but to anticipate and shape it, establishing new industry benchmarks. In the digital era, businesses require shorter response times and increased awareness of market conditions that can shift more rapidly than in previous decades. From this perspective, numerous organizations have been implementing cutting-edge technologies designed to achieve high performance and competitive advantage (Kitsios & Kamariotou, 2021). Among these advancements, Artificial Intelligence (AI) has taken a central role (Akhtar *et al.*, 2019) and has captured the interest of both researchers and industry professionals. AI is defined as a machine's capacity to learn from experience, adapt to new inputs, and perform human-like tasks (Balog, 2019). Researchers (Balog, 2019; Kitsios & Kamariotou, 2021) suggest that AI could now be the innovation with the greatest potential for disruption. Similarly, according to Lichtenthaler (2020), AI is the fundamental multi-purpose technology in the field, particularly concerning machine learning tools. Artificial Intelligence (AI) is generally described as the ability of machines to execute human-like cognitive functions. These can encompass automating physical processes such as manipulating and moving objects, sensing, perceiving, problem-solving, decision-making, and innovation (NewVantage, 2019).

Artificial Intelligence (AI) is currently considered the most significant and transformative emerging technology for major organizations. Nevertheless, its implementation in large enterprises is still in its early stages, and it remains largely absent from smaller businesses, except for tech startups (NewVantage, 2019). Research indicates that less than half of large organizations have substantial AI initiatives in progress, though this proportion is growing over time (Kitsios & Kamariotou, 2021). For most entities, AI projects are primarily experimental, often conducted as pilots or proofs of concept. Few organizations have implemented AI in production environments—an issue explored further in this study. This experimental approach means many organizations have seen little to no financial return on their AI investments. However, some analysts predict that AI adoption will eventually significantly boost company growth and profitability. Organizations are applying AI for various purposes: enhancing process efficiency (28% as one of the top two priorities), improving existing products and services (25%), developing new offerings (23%), enhancing decision-making (21%), and reducing costs (20%) (Deloitte, 2020). Despite frequent media coverage of workforce reduction, this objective received the lowest number of mentions at 11%. Initially, executives focused on leveraging AI technologies to automate specific workflow processes and repetitive tasks. These processes were characterized as linear, stepwise, sequential, and repeatable. This chapter looks at an overview of the AI revolution in strategic management.

Contributions of the Chapter

This chapter explores the transformative effects of artificial intelligence on strategic leadership and management. It examines AI's influence on organizational functions, data analysis, and executive decision-making. Forward-thinking leaders who embrace AI technologies have the chance to transform their business models and operational frameworks, leveraging more precise, real-time data for decision-making. This research breaks new ground by theoretically investigating AI's function in strategic management within the corporate environment. As a result, it contributes to academic discussions and pushes the boundaries of existing knowledge.

LITERATURE

Artificial Intelligence

Artificial Intelligence (AI) has emerged as a crucial component in global organizational operations with its rapid technological advancements (Benbya *et al.*, 2020; Pietronudo *et al.*, 2022). AI is characterized as 'the ability of a machine to perform cognitive functions that we associate with human minds, such as perceiving, reasoning, learning, interacting with the environment, problem-solving, decision-making, and even demonstrating creativity' (Collins *et al.*, 2021). Through extensive databases, sophisticated learning capabilities, and intelligent algorithms, AI enhances managerial decision-making processes, revolutionizing organizational competencies and methodologies (Borges *et al.*, 2021; Krakowski, Luger, & Raisch, 2023; Raisch & Krakowski, 2021). In recent times, generative AI, particularly large-language models, has captured significant managerial interest, prompting executives and boards to integrate these technologies into their digital strategies (Li *et al.*, 2023; Paschen *et al.*, 2020). According to a recent McKinsey investigation report by Hatami and Segel (2023), the introduction of generative AI has been identified as the most significant business development in 2023 (or the past decade), swiftly becoming a top priority for CEOs across thousands of companies. Furthermore, the implementation of AI presents novel opportunities and challenges in the field of organizational strategic management research (Haefner *et al.*, 2021; Von Krogh, 2018). The graphical representation of the study is presented in Fig. (**1**).

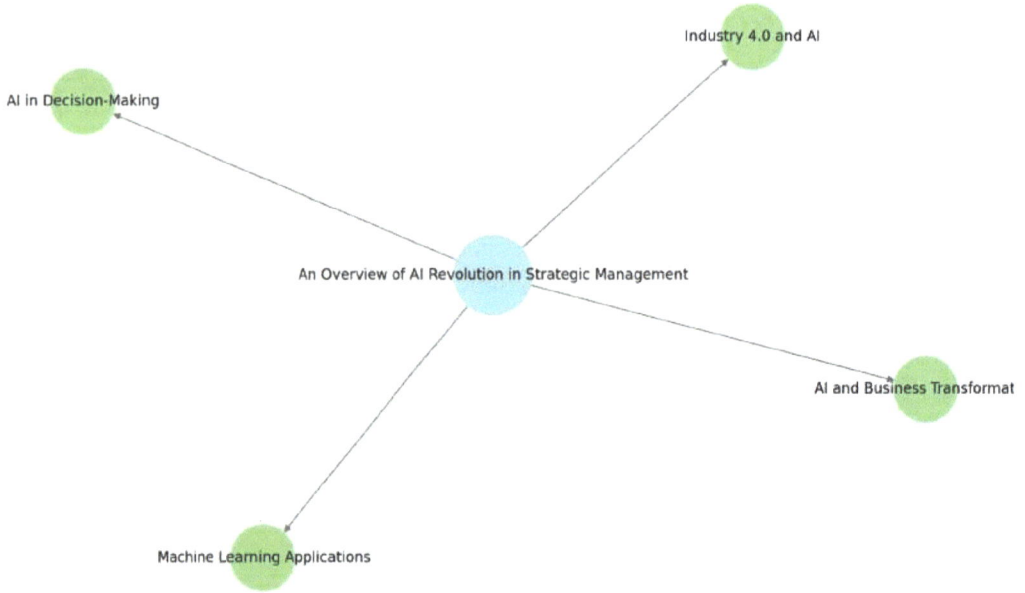

Fig. (1). Conceptual framework.

AI AND STRATEGIC MANAGEMENT

In the current era of technological advancement, Artificial Intelligence (AI) has become ubiquitous in the business world, playing a vital role in various aspects of corporate strategy, including strategic planning, reporting, project management, and organizational alignment. The possibilities are seemingly limitless. For businesses to thrive in today's competitive and rapidly evolving market, effective strategic planning is essential. This process encompasses goal-setting, market analysis, and informed decision-making. The advent of AI technology has transformed the approach businesses take to strategic planning. AI-powered tools and algorithms provide valuable insights, enhance decision-making processes, and boost overall efficiency.

A primary benefit of incorporating AI into strategic planning is its capacity to handle and examine enormous volumes of data. Conventional planning methods often struggle to cope with the vast amount of available information, potentially leading to information overload and overlooking crucial insights (Balog, 2021). AI algorithms excel in analyzing large datasets, identifying meaningful patterns, and generating actionable recommendations. By harnessing AI, companies can gain a comprehensive understanding of market trends, consumer preferences, and competitive landscapes, enabling more informed and effective strategic decisions.

Another area where businesses can leverage AI for strategic planning is through predictive analytics. This technique employs historical data, machine learning algorithms, and statistical modeling to forecast future outcomes. By analyzing patterns and trends in the data, predictive analytics algorithms can generate accurate predictions about consumer behavior, market dynamics, and potential risks and opportunities. This valuable foresight allows businesses to proactively adjust their strategies, identify emerging trends, and maintain a competitive edge (Judijanto *et al.*, 2023).

AI-driven tools can also improve the efficiency and speed of strategic planning processes. Manual analysis and decision-making can be time-consuming and susceptible to human biases. AI algorithms can automate various tasks, such as data collection, processing, and report generation, significantly reducing the time and effort required for strategic planning. This automation allows businesses to allocate more resources to critical thinking and strategic decision-making rather than getting bogged down by repetitive and mundane tasks.

Furthermore, AI can enhance scenario planning, a crucial aspect of strategic planning that involves evaluating multiple future scenarios and their potential impact on the business. AI algorithms can simulate various scenarios based on different assumptions and variables, enabling businesses to assess the risks and opportunities associated with each scenario. This aids in identifying the most favorable course of action and developing contingency plans to mitigate potential risks. By utilizing AI for scenario planning, businesses can make more accurate and data-driven strategic decisions, reducing uncertainty and maximizing their chances of success (Judijanto *et al.*, 2022).

It is important to note, however, that AI should not replace human involvement in strategic planning but rather complement it. While AI algorithms excel at data analysis and generating insights, human judgment, creativity, and intuition remain crucial for effective strategic decision-making.

AI in Strategic Management Process

Artificial Intelligence (AI) provides substantial benefits throughout the strategic planning process, enhancing decision-making and optimizing results at every stage. The following are the key advantages AI brings to the three main phases of strategic management:

- **Strategy Development.**
  - *Information Processing:* AI can analyze extensive datasets from diverse sources, including market dynamics, consumer habits, and rival strategies, offering a holistic perspective for strategy development.

○ *ITrend Identification:* Machine learning algorithms can detect subtle correlations and trends that may escape human notice, yielding more sophisticated strategic insights, such as innovative methods to enhance efficiency and connect with target demographics.

○ Future Forecasting: AI technology can swiftly create and evaluate numerous potential future situations, enabling organizations to prepare for a range of possible outcomes.

○ *Unbiased Decision-making:* The use of AI in strategy formulation minimizes human prejudice, resulting in more impartial and evidence-based choices.

- **Strategy Execution**
  ○ Continuous Performance Tracking: Artificial intelligence platforms can incessantly monitor essential performance metrics and deliver instantaneous updates on the progress of strategy implementation.

  ○ Smart Resource Management: AI technology is capable of flexibly adjusting resource distribution based on shifting circumstances and performance metrics, enhancing the efficiency of strategy execution.

  ○ Anticipatory Analysis: Through AI, potential challenges or prospects during implementation can be anticipated, enabling proactive strategy modifications.

  ○ Computerized Workflow Management: AI has the capacity to streamline routine processes and workflows, allowing human personnel to focus on more intricate, strategic tasks.

- **Strategy Evaluation**
  ○ AI's Multifaceted Evaluation Capabilities: Artificial intelligence can examine and interpret intricate performance datasets to deliver a comprehensive evaluation of strategic efficacy.

  ○ Causal Relationship Detection: Sophisticated AI algorithms are capable of uncovering connections between strategic initiatives and their results, providing a more profound understanding of successful approaches and their rationale.

  ○ Comparative Analysis: AI technology enables organizations to measure their performance against industry norms and rival companies, offering valuable context for strategy assessment.

  ○ Adaptive Improvement: AI systems have the ability to extract lessons from previous strategies and their consequences, leading to ongoing enhancement of the strategic planning process.

  ○ By incorporating AI into these phases, organizations can strengthen their strategic planning process, resulting in more effective strategies, superior implementation, and enhanced long-term performance.

APPLICATIONS OF AI IN STRATEGIC MANAGEMENT

Analyzing Data and Recognizing Patterns

AI's ability to process large datasets and identify hidden patterns surpasses human capabilities. This feature allows organizations to conduct in-depth analyses of market dynamics, consumer habits, and rival tactics with exceptional accuracy. AI algorithms can uncover connections and trends that might be overlooked using conventional methods.

Forecasting with AI

The predictive capabilities of AI enable companies to project future scenarios based on past information. This proves crucial in strategic management, where anticipating market shifts, customer preferences, and potential threats can guide leaders in developing proactive plans. Such forecasting aids in allocating resources, developing products, and managing risks effectively.

AI-enhanced Decision-making

Machine Learning-powered decision support systems assist executives in making well-informed choices. These platforms evaluate data, consider potential outcomes, and provide suggestions, thereby enhancing human decision-making processes. This is particularly valuable in strategic management, where complex decisions require a thorough analysis of multiple factors.

Understanding Human Language

Natural Language Processing (NLP) allows AI systems to comprehend and interpret human communication. In strategic management, this facilitates the examination of text-based information from various sources, including customer feedback, social media posts, and industry publications. By extracting key insights from unstructured data, organizations can develop a comprehensive understanding of market sentiments and industry trends.

Streamlining Repetitive Tasks

AI's automation capabilities optimize routine processes, allowing human resources to concentrate on more strategic aspects of management. Time-consuming and repetitive activities, such as data input and report creation, can be automated, enabling professionals to dedicate their time and expertise to more strategic initiatives.

BENEFITS OF AI IN STRATEGY

Synchronizing OKRs with Overarching Strategic Objectives

Artificial Intelligence can assist in harmonizing Objectives and Key Results (OKRs) with company-wide strategies by evaluating the impact of specific objectives on broader goals and recommending modifications for better alignment. This ensures that each team's efforts contribute to the organization's overall strategic aims (Sailus, 2024). The process of aligning OKRs with strategic objectives requires comprehending the complex interplay between various activities and outcomes across the company. AI's capacity to thoroughly examine these relationships and propose actionable alignments is crucial for effective strategy implementation.

Enhancing Data Processing through AI

Artificial Intelligence provides significant advantages for strategic intelligence, particularly in expediting data processing. AI technologies, such as natural language processing and deep learning algorithms, enable swift analysis of extensive datasets that exceed human capabilities. This not only efficiently addresses complex challenges but also provides prompt insights essential for agile decision-making in dynamic market conditions. By automating data processing and analysis phases, AI shortens the time required to transform raw data into actionable insights, enabling organizations to make more informed decisions quickly. This is especially advantageous in time-sensitive situations, such as reacting to market shifts or emerging threats.

Decision Making

Artificial Intelligence (AI) has become a game-changer across industries, revolutionizing organizational operations and strategic decision-making. In the field of strategic management, AI significantly enhances decision processes, boosts efficiency, and delivers valuable insights. This chapter examines the diverse effects of AI on strategic management, including its applications, advantages, obstacles, and the shifting landscape of AI-driven strategic choices (Jerry, 2024). AI's ability to swiftly process enormous datasets enables it to provide real-time, data-driven insights and predictive analytics, accelerating decisions that previously took weeks. It excels at recognizing patterns, trends, and relationships that might elude human decision-makers, potentially minimizing bias and subjectivity. By furnishing comprehensive data analyses, AI empowers decision-makers to make more informed and timely choices. Considering numerous factors, AI-generated insights contribute to data-grounded strategic decisions, reducing reliance on intuition alone.

Analysis of Vast Datasets

Through the analysis of vast datasets, AI generates instant insights that executives can utilize for decisions on new products, market expansion, investments, and process modifications. While skilled leaders must still outline these strategies, AI tools offer a data-driven foundation. However, it is crucial to recognize that AI lacks human intuition and contextual understanding. Thus, the most effective approach combines AI-generated insights with human expertise and judgment, leveraging the strengths of both artificial and human intelligence for more balanced decision-making.

Idea Generation

In terms of idea generation, AI's extensive training allows it to produce numerous ideas and solutions. When faced with strategic challenges, consulting AI might yield creative solutions that can be incorporated into plans. Nevertheless, it is important to remember that AI's creativity is limited by its training data.

Efficiency

AI also contributes to achieving accuracy and efficiency in market analysis. AI-powered dashboards and reporting tools can distill complex data into actionable insights, facilitating easier comprehension of key strategic metrics for decision-makers and stakeholders. The immense volume and intricacy of data generated by modern businesses necessitate advanced data processing and visualization tools that only AI can efficiently provide, ensuring insights are both accessible and understandable to diverse audiences.

Analysis of Volumes of Data

The influence of Artificial Intelligence (AI) on corporate strategic management is profound. AI's capacity to process vast amounts of data and detect patterns often overlooked by humans leads to enhanced decision-making, more adaptable strategies, and improved business operations (Maksym & Tetiana, 2024). This is primarily accomplished through the automation of both mundane and intricate tasks, which boosts efficiency and cuts expenses. Smart systems can predict production requirements, manage inventory effectively, and oversee supply chains, proving particularly beneficial in dynamic market environments (Hitt & Duhaime, 2021). AI excels at data analysis, trend identification, and uncovering insights that may elude human perception. It can be particularly useful in extracting common themes and unique ideas from interview or focus group data. However, it is crucial to understand AI's reasoning process and ensure it addresses the specific question at hand.

Effectiveness

Artificial Intelligence excels at performing repetitive tasks, processing vast amounts of data swiftly, and providing immediate access to extensive information. This capability proves beneficial for obtaining quick responses for strategic planning, articulating complex concepts, and composing messages for stakeholders.

Data-based Insights

AI possesses the ability to examine massive datasets at speeds and with precision unattainable by humans. This proficiency significantly enhances decision-making processes by uncovering trends, patterns, and irregularities that would be overlooked in manual analysis. In the realm of strategic planning, AI-enhanced analytics assist in identifying patterns and forecasting future outcomes, enabling business leaders to make more informed choices based on accurate predictions. This predictive ability allows companies to distribute resources, handle risks, and plan investments more effectively. As a result, organizations can proactively address challenges and capitalize on opportunities. Executives can ground their business objectives and decisions in solid evidence rather than intuition, minimizing the risk of bias and errors.

Future Scenario Analysis

Artificial Intelligence can propose various potential future situations based on current trends, aiding organizations in preparing for multiple scenarios. While predicting the future with certainty is impossible, this approach can help manage risk by considering various potential challenges that may arise.

Expense Reduction and Efficiency

Businesses that implement Artificial Intelligence can enhance their productivity and decrease their expenses. AI-powered automation in manufacturing and logistics enhances supply chain management and minimizes downtime. In marketing, AI can customize products and services to align with individual customer preferences and address the challenges they encounter.

Automating and Optimizing Task Management

Artificial Intelligence can automate routine tasks, oversee workflows, and prioritize tasks based on urgency and resource availability. This reduces human error, boosts efficiency, and allows employees to concentrate on more strategic activities (Hamadaga *et al.*, 2024). AI-driven automation not only accelerates processes but also introduces intelligence to task management, such as predictive task scheduling and optimization, which are not feasible on a large scale without AI.

Streamlining Repetitive Processes

Artificial Intelligence streamlines numerous repetitive tasks, allowing strategists to dedicate their efforts to more intricate, theoretical, and imaginative aspects of their responsibilities. This streamlining enables companies to function more effectively and make strategic decisions more rapidly and assuredly.

Obtaining Instantaneous Insights on Performance Patterns

Artificial Intelligence can examine large amounts of information from various origins in real-time, enabling businesses to swiftly recognize patterns, irregularities, and prospects. This immediate understanding permits companies to make well-informed choices promptly, adjusting to market shifts or operational requirements as they emerge (Hamadaga *et al.*, 2024).

Forecasting Abilities

Artificial Intelligence predicts future patterns and obstacles, enabling companies to simulate various scenarios and offering strategic foresight that is invaluable in a rapidly evolving market. This proactive approach assists businesses in staying ahead of competitors and addressing potential issues before they become critical.

Acquiring Customized Strategic Guidance

Artificial Intelligence systems can customize recommendations by learning from data related to business performance, market conditions, and individual preferences. These tailored strategies assist businesses in optimizing operations and enhancing decision-making processes (Hamadaga *et al.*, 2024). The intricacy and variability of data involved in developing strategic recommendations surpass the capabilities of conventional analytical methods. Artificial Intelligence's learning abilities enable it to provide nuanced insights that are specifically aligned with a company's unique objectives and contexts.

Enhanced Productivity

The automation of routine tasks not only conserves time but also diminishes the probability of errors associated with manual processes. This productivity gain allows organizations to strategically reallocate resources, fostering efficiency and competitiveness.

Competitive Edge

Organizations that effectively incorporate Artificial Intelligence into their strategic management processes gain a competitive advantage. The ability to swiftly analyze data, forecast market trends, and adapt to changing circumstances positions these entities to respond more effectively to market dynamics.

OBSTACLES IN APPLYING AI TO STRATEGIC MANAGEMENT

Data Integrity and Confidentiality Issues: AI systems' efficacy relies on the integrity of the data they process. Subpar data can result in erroneous insights and misguided decision-making. Moreover, the utilization of extensive datasets raises privacy concerns, demanding robust data management and ethical considerations (Jerry, 2024).

Complexity of System Integration: Incorporating AI into current strategic management frameworks can be intricate. Organizations might encounter difficulties in modifying legacy systems, ensuring compatibility, and providing sufficient staff training. Surmounting these integration challenges is vital for the smooth incorporation of AI into strategic processes.

Insufficient Comprehension and Confidence: Some decision-makers may be reluctant to depend on AI-generated insights due to limited understanding or skepticism towards the technology. Increasing awareness, cultivating a data-driven decision-making culture, and showcasing the dependability of AI systems are crucial for overcoming these obstacles.

Legal and Moral Considerations: As AI becomes more widespread in strategic management, regulatory frameworks and ethical issues gain importance. Ensuring adherence to data protection regulations, addressing algorithmic bias, and maintaining ethical standards are crucial aspects of responsible AI implementation.

ROLE OF ARTIFICIAL INTELLIGENCE AND STRATEGIC MANAGEMENT

The role of Artificial Intelligence in strategic management is dynamic and multifaceted. From data analysis and predictive analytics to decision support systems and automation, AI offers a myriad of tools that can significantly enhance the strategic decision-making processes of organizations. While the benefits are substantial, challenges related to data quality, integration complexity, and ethical considerations must be carefully addressed.

AI Aspects in Strategic Management

Strategic management is being revolutionized by Artificial Intelligence, which is transforming the way companies develop, implement, and assess their strategies through the facilitation of data-driven decision-making processes.

Leveraging AI in Strategic Planning

The foundation for a company's future success is laid through strategic planning, which guides decision-making and resource distribution. The integration of AI into this process enhances its effectiveness, predictability, and flexibility (Middleton, 2024). AI's capacity to swiftly analyze extensive data sets and generate actionable insights revolutionizes strategic planning. It helps identify market patterns, forecast consumer behaviors, and anticipate potential obstacles, allowing businesses to make proactive, data-driven choices (Middleton, 2024). Furthermore, AI-driven predictive analytics can assist companies in aligning their strategies with future market conditions, providing them with a competitive edge.

AI's Role in Business Reporting

A crucial component of strategic management is business reporting, which offers valuable insights into company performance. Traditional reporting methods, however, are often slow and prone to errors. AI enhances this process by automating data gathering, processing, and analysis. It can produce real-time reports and detect trends or anomalies, facilitating faster and more precise decision-making.

Implementing AI in Project Management

Project management is often a complex and demanding task, requiring careful coordination, planning, and execution. AI simplifies these processes by assisting with task allocation, resource management, risk assessment, and performance monitoring. It can also aid in scenario planning, enabling project managers to foresee potential issues and proactively implement mitigation strategies (Middleton, 2024).

Utilizing AI for Organizational Alignment

Ensuring that all members of an organization are working towards common goals is the essence of organizational alignment. AI can promote this alignment by enhancing communication, encouraging collaboration, and providing clear visibility into objectives and progress. AI-powered tools can help keep team members informed and engaged, which is essential for alignment (Middleton, 2024). These tools can also track progress in real time, identify areas where alignment is lacking, and recommend corrective actions, ensuring all departments and teams are working in harmony.

CONCLUSION

AI is no longer an optional add-on but a necessary tool for strategic planning, reporting, project management, and organizational alignment. As the landscape of AI continues to evolve, organizations that successfully integrate and leverage AI in their strategic management practices stand to gain a competitive advantage. The future likely involves not only the continuous refinement of AI technologies but also a harmonious collaboration between human expertise and artificial intelligence, shaping a new era of strategic management. With technology like AI, companies can harness the power of AI to make their processes more efficient, predictive, and aligned. Investing in AI-powered solutions not only streamlines operations but also helps businesses stay ahead of the curve in today's rapidly evolving market. As firms continue to push the boundaries of what AI can do, one thing is clear: AI is transforming the way business strategy is managed, and companies that leverage its capabilities will lead the way forward.

REFERENCES

Akhtar, P., Frynas, J.G., Mellahi, K., Ullah, S. (2019). Big data-savvy teams' skills, big data-driven actions and business performance. *British Journal of Management, 30*(2), 252-271.
[http://dx.doi.org/10.1111/1467-8551.12333]

Balog, K. (2020). The concept and competitiveness of agile organization in the fourth industrial revolution's drift. *Strategic Management, 25*(3), 14-27.
[http://dx.doi.org/10.5937/StraMan2003014B]

Balog, K. (2021). Conversational AI from an information retrieval perspective: Remaining challenges and a case for user simulation. 2nd International Conference on Design of Experimental Search & Information REtrieval Systems, September 15–18, 2021, Padua, Italy.

Benbya, H., Davenport, TH, Pachidi, S. (2020). Artificial intelligence in organizations: Current state and future opportunities. *MIS Quarterly Executive, 19*(4) Article 4 Available at SSRN: https://ssrn.com/abstract=3741983 or http://dx.doi.org/10.2139/ssrn.3741983

Borges, A.F.S., Laurindo, F.J.B., Spínola, M.M., Gonçalves, R.F., Mattos, C.A. (2021). The strategic use of artificial intelligence in the digital era: Systematic literature review and future research directions. *International journal of information management, 57*, 102225.
[http://dx.doi.org/10.1016/j.ijinfomgt.2020.102225]

Collins, P.H., da Silva, E.C.G., Ergun, E., Furseth, I., Bond, K.D., Martínez-Palacios, J. (2021). Intersectionality as critical social theory: Intersectionality as critical social theory, Patricia Hill Collins, Duke University Press, 2019. *Contemporary Political Theory, 20*(3), 690.
[http://dx.doi.org/10.1057/s41296-021-00490-0]

Deloitte. (2020). Thriving in the era of pervasive AI: Deloitte's state of AI in the enterprise, 3rd edition. Deloitte Insights. Available from: https://www2.deloitte.com/us/en/insights/focus/cognitive-technologies/state-of-ai-and-intelligent-automation-in-business-survey.html.

Haefner, N., Wincent, J., Parida, V., Gassmann, O. (2021). Artificial intelligence and innovation management: A review, framework, and research agenda. *Technological Forecasting and Social Change, 162*, 120392.

[http://dx.doi.org/10.1016/j.techfore.2020.120392]

Hitt, M.A., Duhaime, I.M., Lyles, M.A. (2021). *Strategic management: State of the field and its future..* Oxford University Press.

Jerry. (2024, January 31). The role of artificial intelligence in strategic management. Available from: https://www.topmanagement.net/the-role-of-artificial-intelligence-in-strategic-management/.

Judijanto,L., Asfahani. A., Bakri, A.A.Susanto, E. &Kulsum,U.(2022).AI-supported management through leveraging artificial intelligence for effective decision making. *Journal of Artificial Intelligence and Development.* *1*(1), 59-68.

Kitsios, F., Kamariotou, M. (2021). Artificial intelligence and business strategy towards digital transformation: A research agenda. *Sustainability,* *13*(4), 2025. [http://dx.doi.org/10.3390/su13042025]

Krakowski, S., Luger, J., Raisch, S. (2023). Artificial intelligence and the changing sources of competitive advantage. *Strategic Management Journal,* *44*(6), 1425-1452. [http://dx.doi.org/10.1002/smj.3387]

Lichtenthaler, U. (2020). Building blocks of successful digital transformation: Complementing technology and market issues. *International Journal of Innovation and Technology Management,* *17*.

Li, N., Wang, X., Zhang, S. (2023). Effects of digitization on enterprise growth performance: Mediating role of strategic change and moderating role of dynamic capability. *Managerial and Decision Economics,* *44*(2), 1040-1053. [http://dx.doi.org/10.1002/mde.3730]

McKinsey & Co. (2018). Notes from the AI frontier: Modeling the impact of AI on the world economy. Available from: https://www.mckinsey.com/featured-insights/artificial-intelligence/notes-from-the-ai-frontier-modeling-the-impact-of-ai-on-the-world-economy# Middleton.

Middleton, A. (2024, August 19). AI in performance management: How AI can support leaders. Available from: https://www.clearpointstrategy.com/blog/ai-performance-management.

NewVantage. (2019). Big data and AI executive survey 2019, executive summary of findings. NewVantage Partners. Available from: https://newvantage.com/wp-content/uploads/2018/12/Big-Data-Executive-.

Paschen, U., Pitt, C., Kietzmann, J. (2020). Artificial intelligence: Building blocks and an innovation typology. *Business Horizons,* *63*(2), 147-155. [http://dx.doi.org/10.1016/j.bushor.2019.10.004]

Pietronudo, M.C., Croidieu, G., Schiavone, F. (2022). A solution looking for problems? A systematic literature review of the rationalizing influence of artificial intelligence on decision-making in innovation management. *Technological Forecasting and Social Change,* *182*, 121828. [http://dx.doi.org/10.1016/j.techfore.2022.121828]

Raisch, S., Krakowski, S. (2021). Artificial intelligence and management: The automation–augmentation paradox. *Academy of management review,* *46*(1), 192-210. Survey-2019-Findings-Updated-010219-1.pdf [http://dx.doi.org/10.5465/amr.2018.0072]

Von Krogh, G. (2018). Artificial intelligence in organizations: New opportunities for phenomenon-based theorizing. *Academy of Management Discoveries,* *4*(4), 404-409. [http://dx.doi.org/10.5465/amd.2018.0084]

CHAPTER 2

Building an AI-ready Organization: Culture, Talent, and Leadership

Abstract: This chapter explores the multifaceted aspects of building an AI-ready organization, focusing on the interdependencies between culture, talent, and leadership. The findings indicate that organizational culture plays a critical role in AI adoption. A culture that fosters innovation, collaboration, and agility enables organizations to effectively embrace AI technologies while overcoming resistance to change. Additionally, talent development is essential for AI readiness. Organizations must not only acquire new AI-skilled talent but also prioritize upskilling and reskilling existing employees to adapt to evolving technologies. Establishing a learning culture that promotes continuous education is fundamental for maintaining competitiveness in the AI era. Leadership also emerges as a pivotal factor in AI integration. Visionary leaders must align AI initiatives with strategic business goals while fostering cross-functional collaboration. Furthermore, ethical considerations in AI adoption highlight the importance of responsible AI governance to ensure transparency, fairness, and accountability in AI implementation.

Keywords: AI, AI-ready, Culture, Leadership, Talent, Technology.

INTRODUCTION

In an era where Artificial Intelligence (AI) is fundamentally transforming industries and redefining business practices, the importance of cultivating an AI-ready organization cannot be overstated. As organizations increasingly recognize that successful AI implementation extends beyond merely investing in advanced technologies, they are coming to understand that it necessitates a holistic transformation encompassing culture, talent, and leadership. Building an AI-ready organization is not just about adopting new tools; it involves fostering an environment that embraces innovation, encourages continuous learning, and equips employees with the necessary skills to leverage AI effectively. At the heart of this transformation lies organizational culture, which serves as the foundation for successful AI adoption. An organization's culture influences how employees perceive change, interact with new technologies, and approach problem-solving. A culture that values experimentation, agility, and collaboration is essential for organizations aiming to harness the full potential of AI technologies. In such an environment, employees are more likely to engage with AI-driven tools and processes, exploring innovative applications that can lead to improved efficiency and better decision-making. Moreover, fostering a culture of psychological safety where employees feel free to voice their ideas and concerns can significantly enhance the organization's ability to adapt to the rapid changes associated with AI integration (Wang *et al.*, 2023).

Talent is another critical component in building an AI-ready organization. As AI technologies continue to evolve, the demand for skilled professionals who can design, implement, and manage AI systems has surged (Castrounis, 2019). Organizations must prioritize attracting and retaining talent with the necessary expertise in data science, machine learning, and AI ethics. The skillset required for AI-driven roles is often multidisciplinary, combining technical expertise with a deep understanding of business processes and ethical considerations. Therefore, organizations need to implement comprehensive talent acquisition strategies that not only target traditional tech hubs but also consider diverse educational backgrounds and experiences (Dhasarathy *et al.*, 2020). Furthermore, investing in the upskilling and reskilling of existing employees is essential to ensure that the workforce is prepared to adapt to the demands of an AI-driven landscape. Training programs that focus on AI literacy, data analysis, and critical thinking can empower employees to leverage AI tools effectively in their respective roles. Additionally, organizations should create mentorship and coaching programs to facilitate knowledge transfer and skill development, fostering a culture of continuous learning that is vital for sustaining competitive advantage (Fenwick *et al.*, 2024).

Leadership plays a pivotal role in steering organizations toward an AI-ready future. Leaders must not only champion the adoption of AI but also communicate a clear vision that aligns AI initiatives with the organization's strategic goals. This includes setting realistic expectations for AI capabilities and encouraging a mindset that embraces change and innovation. Effective leaders promote cross-functional collaboration, breaking down silos that often impede the flow of information and ideas. By fostering an environment where diverse teams can collaborate on AI projects, leaders can facilitate the integration of AI into various business functions, ensuring that the organization is well-positioned to navigate the complexities of the digital age (Henk and Nilssen, 2021).

This chapter delves into the multifaceted aspects of building an AI-ready organization, exploring the interdependencies between culture, talent, and leadership. It aims to provide insights and practical strategies for organizations seeking to embrace AI as a core component of their operations, ultimately enabling them to thrive in an increasingly competitive and technology-driven marketplace. The study's graphical representation is shown in Fig. (**1**) below.

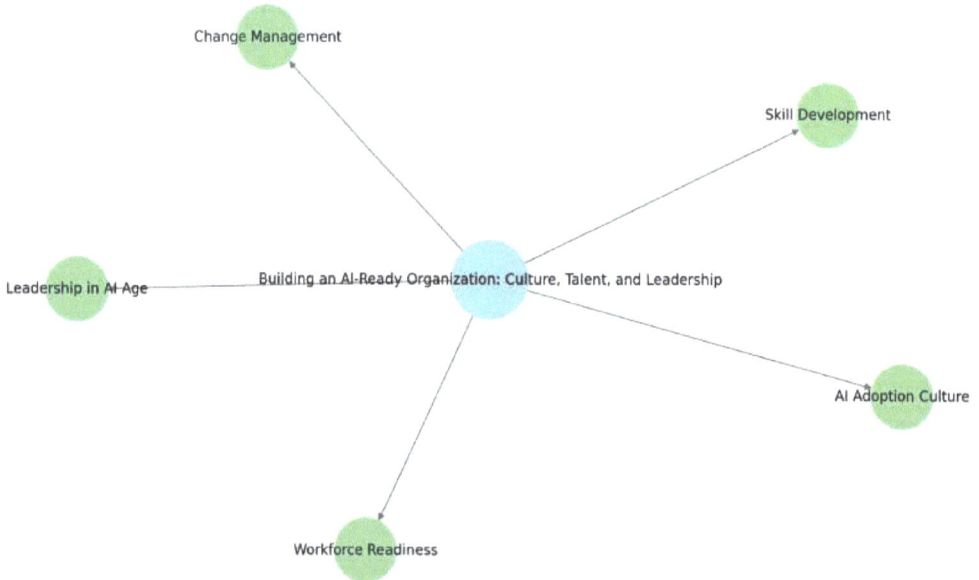

Fig. (1). Conceptual framework.

INTRODUCTION TO BUILDING AN AI-READY ORGANIZATION

The rise of Artificial Intelligence (AI) has brought about transformative changes across industries, prompting organizations to adopt AI technologies as a means of remaining competitive, as shown in Fig. (**1**). However, the mere integration of AI tools into operations is insufficient for long-term success. To fully harness the potential of AI, organizations must become AI-ready, which involves more than just technology. It encompasses changes in culture, talent development, and leadership. An AI-ready organization is one that has the strategic, structural, and human resources necessary to effectively integrate AI into its decision-making processes, operations, and innovation efforts.

Definition and Importance of an AI-ready Organization

An AI-ready organization can be defined as one that has aligned its technological infrastructure, human capital, and leadership strategies to fully support the integration and utilization of AI in its business processes. AI readiness goes beyond implementing AI systems; it involves preparing the workforce to work with AI, fostering a culture that embraces innovation, and developing leaders capable of guiding the organization through AI-related changes. Organizations that succeed in becoming AI-ready can better respond to shifts in the competitive landscape, increase operational efficiency, and unlock new opportunities for growth and innovation (Polisetty *et al.*, 2024). The importance of AI readiness lies in its ability to enhance the adaptability and resilience of businesses in a rapidly evolving technological landscape. As AI continues to drive automation, data analysis, and process optimization, organizations that are prepared to integrate these technologies will be better positioned to outperform their competitors. Moreover, AI readiness ensures that businesses can capitalize on the benefits of AI while mitigating the risks associated with improper implementation, such as ethical concerns, workforce displacement, and strategic misalignment (Tehrani *et al.*, 2024).

KEY COMPONENTS: CULTURE, TALENT, AND LEADERSHIP

Building an AI-ready organization revolves around three key components: culture, talent, and leadership. Each of these elements plays a crucial role in ensuring that AI integration is both effective and sustainable.

Culture

Organizational culture is the backbone of successful AI adoption. A culture that fosters innovation, agility, and experimentation is necessary to overcome the challenges associated with implementing AI. Organizations with a forward-thinking culture encourage employees to embrace AI as a tool for improvement rather than a threat to their roles. This shift in mindset is critical to promoting collaboration between AI technologies and human workers, thereby leading to enhanced creativity and problem-solving capabilities (Randriamiary, 2024).

Talent

In addition to a supportive culture, talent development is a key driver of AI readiness. Organizations must not only attract individuals with specialized skills in AI, data science, and machine learning but also invest in the continuous development of their existing workforce. Upskilling and reskilling programs are essential to ensure that employees are prepared to work alongside AI systems and utilize them to enhance their performance. The demand for AI specialists is growing, and organizations that can cultivate this talent internally will gain a significant competitive advantage (Hansen *et al.*, 2024).

Leadership

Effective leadership is the third critical component of building an AI-ready organization. Leaders play a pivotal role in setting the strategic direction for AI adoption, fostering a culture of innovation, and guiding the organization through the challenges of transformation. AI readiness requires leaders who are not only knowledgeable about AI technologies but also capable of aligning AI initiatives with the broader strategic goals of the organization. Leaders must communicate a clear vision for AI integration, champion collaboration across departments, and ensure that the organization remains adaptable in the face of technological advancements (Whitlock and Strickland, 2022).

THE SIGNIFICANCE OF AI READINESS IN MODERN BUSINESS TRANSFORMATION

In today's fast-paced and highly competitive business environment, the ability to adapt to emerging technologies, such as AI, is a defining factor for success. AI is rapidly becoming a driving force in areas such as automation, data-driven decision-making, and personalized customer experiences. As such, organizations that are not prepared for AI integration risk falling behind their competitors. According to a study by McKinsey, companies that are early adopters of AI have the potential to increase their cash flow by over 120% by 2030 compared to companies that are slower to integrate these technologies (Jöhnk *et al.*, 2021).

AI readiness is not only about staying competitive; it also contributes to long-term business sustainability. Organizations that are equipped to manage AI-driven transformations can optimize their operations, reduce costs, and unlock new revenue streams. Furthermore, AI enables businesses to anticipate market trends, respond to customer needs more effectively, and innovate faster. This makes AI readiness a strategic imperative for organizations seeking to thrive in the digital age.

In conclusion, building an AI-ready organization requires a comprehensive approach that includes cultivating a culture of innovation, developing AI-specific talent, and ensuring strong leadership. As AI continues to evolve and disrupt industries, organizations that prioritize AI readiness will be better positioned to capitalize on its potential for driving business transformation.

ORGANIZATIONAL CULTURE AND AI ADOPTION

The adoption of Artificial Intelligence (AI) within organizations extends far beyond simply acquiring the technology. A critical factor in the successful integration of AI lies in an organization's culture. Organizational culture defines the shared values, beliefs, and behaviors that guide how employees interact with each other and approach their work. It is a powerful determinant of whether AI is embraced as an opportunity for innovation or resisted as a threat. Therefore, fostering a culture that supports AI adoption is crucial for businesses seeking to leverage AI for long-term success.

The Role of Organizational Culture in Fostering AI Integration

The integration of AI into business processes requires a fundamental shift in how organizations operate. This transformation can only be achieved if an organization's culture aligns with the strategic goals of AI adoption. An AI-supportive culture encourages employees to embrace the opportunities that AI presents rather than fear potential disruptions to their roles. It also promotes a mindset that views AI as a tool to enhance decision-making and productivity rather than a competitor to human capabilities (Chen *et al.*, 2021). AI integration involves a continuous learning curve. As employees work alongside AI systems, their ability to adapt, collaborate, and innovate becomes essential. In this context, organizational culture plays a pivotal role in driving AI-related change, fostering openness to new technologies, and enabling collaboration across different teams and departments. Moreover, leaders within organizations that prioritize an AI-supportive culture can help minimize resistance and champion the use of AI as a strategic asset.

Characteristics of an AI-Supportive Culture

For AI adoption to thrive, certain cultural traits must be embedded within the organization:

- **Innovation:** An AI-supportive culture is one that encourages experimentation and innovation. Organizations that value creativity and exploration are more likely to adopt AI technologies and experiment with their potential applications across different areas of the business. These companies foster an environment where failure is seen as an opportunity for learning, which is essential for embracing cutting-edge technologies like AI (Kulkov *et al.*, 2024).
- **Agility:** The pace of technological advancement in AI is rapid, and organizations need to remain agile to keep up. Agility in this context refers to the ability to quickly adapt to changes in technology, market demands, and industry trends. Organizations with agile cultures can rapidly implement AI solutions and adjust their strategies as AI capabilities evolve. Such flexibility is crucial for continuous improvement and staying competitive in a dynamic business environment (Enholm *et al.*, 2022).
- **Collaboration:** AI adoption often requires cross-functional collaboration between IT, data science, operations, and other business units. A culture that promotes teamwork and knowledge-sharing ensures that different departments can work together to implement AI solutions effectively. Collaboration is also

essential for integrating human insights with AI-driven data analytics, creating a harmonious balance between AI and human intelligence in decision-making (Jöhnk *et al.*, 2021).

Cultural Resistance to AI and Strategies to Overcome It

Despite the potential benefits of AI, resistance to its adoption is common in many organizations. Cultural resistance often stems from fear of the unknown, particularly concerns about job displacement and the perception that AI will replace human workers. Additionally, employees may feel that AI threatens their autonomy or the established processes they are accustomed to. This resistance can manifest as reluctance to engage with AI technologies, reduced morale, or outright opposition to AI-related changes (Mikalef and Gupta, 2021).

To overcome cultural resistance, organizations need to implement several strategies:

- **Education and Transparency:** Providing employees with clear information about how AI will be used and what its implications are for their roles can help reduce fears. Transparency around the objectives of AI adoption and its potential to complement human work can build trust and engagement (Chaudhuri *et al.*, 2024).
- **Involvement and Inclusion:** Involving employees in the AI adoption process by seeking their input and feedback helps to foster a sense of ownership over the changes. Employees who feel that their perspectives are valued are more likely to support the integration of AI into their workflows (Pillai and Sivathanu, 2020).
- **Change Management:** Effective change management practices are critical to easing the transition to an AI-driven culture. This involves clear communication from leadership, consistent messaging about the benefits of AI, and support systems, such as training programs, to help employees adapt to new AI tools (Pillai and Sivathanu, 2020).
- **Upskilling and Reskilling:** To mitigate fears of job loss, organizations can focus on upskilling and reskilling employees, providing them with the necessary knowledge and competencies to work effectively with AI. This not only enhances employee confidence but also ensures that the organization maximizes the potential of both AI and human talent (Chowdhury *et al.*, 2023).

Case Studies: Companies with Successful AI-driven Cultures

Several companies have demonstrated success in integrating AI into their operations by fostering cultures that support innovation, agility, and collaboration. For example:

- **Amazon:** Amazon's culture is deeply rooted in innovation, allowing the company to lead in the application of AI technologies. Amazon uses AI to optimize its supply chain, personalize customer recommendations, and power its virtual assistant, Alexa. The company's willingness to experiment with AI across different areas of its business reflects a strong innovation-driven culture (Fountaine *et al.*, 2019).

- **Google:** Google has developed an agile culture that emphasizes continuous learning and experimentation with AI. Google's AI research arm, DeepMind, has been instrumental in advancing AI technologies, particularly in areas such as natural language processing and machine learning. The company encourages collaboration between its AI teams and other departments to ensure that AI solutions are integrated seamlessly into its core products and services (Venkatesh, 2022).

- **Netflix:** Netflix's use of AI to enhance its content recommendation system is a prime example of an AI-supportive culture at work. The company's collaborative approach ensures that data scientists, product managers, and content creators work together to fine-tune AI algorithms that personalize the viewing experience for its users. This integration of AI into decision-making processes has helped Netflix maintain a competitive edge in the entertainment industry (Shrestha *et al.*, 2019).

In conclusion, organizational culture plays a fundamental role in determining the success of AI adoption. Companies that embrace a culture of innovation, agility, and collaboration are more likely to integrate AI effectively, driving improvements in productivity, decision-making, and long-term competitiveness.

TALENT DEVELOPMENT FOR AI COMPETENCY

In the era of Artificial Intelligence (AI), the development of talent skilled in AI technologies has become a crucial driver of competitive advantage. As businesses increasingly rely on AI for decision-making, product innovation, and operational efficiency, the demand for professionals with AI expertise has grown exponentially. However, acquiring and developing talent capable of working with AI presents a significant challenge for many organizations. To remain competitive, companies must focus on talent acquisition, upskilling, and fostering a culture of continuous learning that supports AI readiness.

The Growing Demand for AI-related Skills and Expertise

The rapid advancements in AI technologies, including machine learning, natural language processing, and data analytics, have created a demand for a workforce with specialized AI skills. According to (Faqihi and Miah, 2023), roles such as AI specialists, data scientists, and machine learning engineers are among the fastest-growing job categories globally. This demand reflects the increasing adoption of AI across industries, from healthcare and finance to manufacturing and retail.

However, the supply of AI talent has not kept pace with demand. The global shortage of AI professionals has led to fierce competition among organizations for individuals with the necessary skills to design, implement, and maintain AI systems. As a result, companies are not only competing in terms of technology but also in their ability to attract and retain top AI talent (Khang, 2024).

Talent Acquisition: Sourcing and Retaining AI Professionals

Acquiring AI talent requires organizations to rethink traditional hiring practices and adopt strategies that target individuals with the right mix of technical skills and innovation-oriented mindsets. Companies must source talent from diverse fields, including computer science, data analytics, and engineering, while also considering candidates with interdisciplinary expertise in areas such as business strategy and behavioral sciences (Lilly *et al.*, 2022).

To attract AI professionals, organizations must offer competitive compensation packages, invest in cutting-edge AI technologies, and provide opportunities for career growth and continuous learning. Tech giants such as Google, Facebook, and Amazon have built their AI dominance in part by offering top-tier benefits and fostering dynamic, research-driven environments that appeal to AI professionals (Malik *et al.*, 2021).

Retention is equally important, as organizations must work to keep AI talent engaged. Providing AI experts with meaningful projects that challenge their abilities and offering them autonomy in problem-solving can reduce turnover. Additionally, creating clear pathways for career progression within AI roles helps to ensure that professionals stay committed to the organization in the long term (Paramita, 2020).

Upskilling and Reskilling: Training Existing Employees in AI Tools and Technologies

While talent acquisition is important, organizations must also invest in upskilling and reskilling their current workforce to bridge the AI skills gap. Upskilling refers to the process of training employees to gain new skills in AI-related areas while reskilling focuses on enabling employees to transition from non-AI roles into positions that require AI expertise. This strategy is particularly important for organizations seeking to harness the potential of AI without relying solely on external hires.

Training programs that focus on data literacy, coding, machine learning algorithms, and AI ethics can empower employees to contribute to AI initiatives within their organizations. These programs can be delivered through a variety of formats, including online courses, boot camps, and workshops, often in partnership with educational institutions or AI technology providers (Shen, 2022). For example, companies such as IBM and Microsoft have created internal AI academies to upskill their workforce and prepare employees for AI-driven business transformations (Odugbesan *et al.*, 2023).

Additionally, reskilling initiatives can help employees transition into AI-related roles by providing them with the foundational knowledge needed to work with AI technologies. This not only addresses the talent shortage but also helps organizations avoid potential layoffs as AI automates certain job functions. Companies that proactively reskill their workforce in AI-related fields can build a more agile and adaptable organization (Yanamala, 2024).

Creating a Learning Culture that Supports AI Readiness

An organization's culture plays a critical role in enabling successful AI adoption, particularly when it comes to talent development. Building an AI-ready organization requires a culture that encourages continuous learning, experimentation, and collaboration. In this environment, employees are motivated to expand their knowledge, stay updated on the latest AI trends, and embrace new tools and technologies (Rožman *et al.*, 2022).

Creating a learning culture begins with leadership that prioritizes talent development as a strategic objective. This involves providing employees with the resources and time to pursue learning opportunities, whether through formal training programs or self-directed study. Leaders should also promote cross-functional collaboration between AI teams and other departments, ensuring that employees from various areas of the organization can learn from each other and contribute to AI initiatives (Mishra *et al.*, 2020).

Encouraging experimentation with AI technologies is another important aspect of a learning culture. Employees should feel empowered to explore the potential applications of AI within their own areas of responsibility, even if the outcomes are uncertain. By fostering a culture of innovation, organizations can drive AI competency across the workforce and develop a competitive edge in the market.

Examples of Companies Building AI-Focused Talent Pools

Several organizations have successfully built AI-focused talent pools by prioritizing talent acquisition, upskilling, and a strong learning culture:

- **Microsoft:** Microsoft has invested heavily in AI talent development through its AI Business School, which offers employees and customers training in AI strategy, leadership, and ethics. This initiative is part of the company's broader

  commitment to AI readiness, ensuring that employees at all levels understand how to work with AI technologies (Ogbeibu *et al.*, 2022).
- **IBM:** IBM has launched an AI Skills Academy to train its employees in AI-related skills. The program offers hands-on training in areas such as machine learning, natural language processing, and AI ethics. IBM's focus on upskilling has enabled the company to remain a leader in AI innovation, even as the demand for AI talent increases (Pathak and Solanki, 2021).
- **Accenture:** Accenture has taken a proactive approach to talent development by offering AI training to both technical and non-technical employees. The company's AI apprenticeship program aims to reskill individuals from diverse backgrounds, allowing them to transition into AI-related roles within the organization. This strategy has enabled Accenture to build a robust AI talent pool while addressing workforce diversity (Carrel, 2019).

By focusing on talent acquisition, upskilling, and creating a learning culture, organizations can develop the AI competency necessary to drive innovation and maintain a competitive advantage in the digital age.

LEADERSHIP IN AI-DRIVEN ORGANIZATIONS

As organizations increasingly turn to Artificial Intelligence (AI) to drive innovation and gain competitive advantage, the role of leadership becomes paramount. Leadership in AI-driven organizations not only involves overseeing the adoption of AI technologies but also guiding the entire organization through the transformation process. Effective leaders must be visionary, able to align AI with long-term business goals, and foster a culture of cross-functional collaboration and continuous innovation. This section explores the critical role leadership plays in AI adoption, strategies for promoting innovation and managing change, and case studies of successful AI-driven leadership.

The Role of Leadership in AI Adoption and Organizational Transformation

The success of AI integration in an organization is heavily influenced by the leadership's ability to set a clear direction and facilitate change. Leaders must not only champion the adoption of AI technologies but also navigate the complexities of integrating these systems into existing business processes. According to Malik *et al.* (2021), strong leadership is one of the key factors that determine whether an AI transformation will succeed or fail. Leaders must establish a vision for how AI can enhance organizational performance and guide employees through the inevitable disruptions that AI will cause.

Leadership in AI-driven organizations also involves fostering a mindset of learning and experimentation. AI technologies are rapidly evolving, and organizations must adapt quickly to stay competitive. Leaders who encourage a culture of learning and flexibility empower their teams to explore new AI applications, test innovative solutions, and iterate on ideas without fear of failure (Schiff *et al.*, 2020). This leadership approach is crucial for maintaining an organization's agility in the face of technological change.

Visionary Leadership and Aligning AI with Strategic Business Goals

Visionary leaders play a crucial role in aligning AI initiatives with an organization's broader strategic goals. By articulating a clear vision for AI adoption, leaders can inspire employees and stakeholders to embrace AI as a core component of the organization's future. Leaders must be able to identify the long-term potential of AI and communicate how these technologies can transform business operations, improve customer experiences, and unlock new growth opportunities.

Leaders who effectively integrate AI into their organization's strategic goals ensure that AI initiatives are not just isolated projects but are embedded in the organization's overall business strategy. This involves setting clear objectives for AI investments, defining measurable outcomes, and ensuring that AI initiatives align with Key Performance Indicators (KPIs) (Allioui and Mourdi, 2023). By doing so, leaders can maximize the value of AI for the business and position the organization for sustained competitive advantage.

Encouraging Cross-functional Collaboration for AI Success

AI adoption often requires collaboration between various departments, such as IT, data science, marketing, and operations. Leaders must facilitate cross-functional collaboration to ensure that AI initiatives are integrated seamlessly across the organization. This collaborative approach helps break down silos and enables different teams to leverage their expertise to optimize AI systems for different business functions (Kulkov *et al.*, 2024).

In an AI-driven organization, cross-functional teams should work together to identify AI use cases, develop data-driven strategies, and implement AI solutions. Leadership plays a key role in creating the structures and communication channels that allow these teams to collaborate effectively. By fostering a culture of teamwork and openness, leaders can ensure that AI initiatives are supported by diverse perspectives and expertise, increasing the likelihood of success (Füller *et al.*, 2022).

Leadership Strategies to Promote Innovation and Manage Change in AI Adoption

The adoption of AI technologies often requires significant changes to business processes, roles, and organizational structures. Effective leadership is crucial for managing this change and ensuring that employees are prepared for the transition. Leaders must employ strategies that promote innovation while addressing potential resistance to AI adoption.

One key strategy is to create a sense of urgency around AI adoption by highlighting the competitive advantages that AI can bring. Leaders can inspire employees by showcasing how AI can enhance productivity, drive innovation, and improve business outcomes (Jöhnk *et al.*, 2021). Additionally, leaders should be transparent about the potential challenges of AI adoption and provide support, such as training programs, to help employees acquire the necessary skills to work with AI technologies.

Change management is another important aspect of leadership in AI adoption. Leaders must be proactive in addressing employee concerns about AI, such as fears of job displacement or the complexity of AI tools. By fostering a culture of open communication, leaders can alleviate these concerns and build trust within the organization. Engaging employees early in the AI adoption process and involving them in decision-making can also reduce resistance and create a sense of ownership over AI initiatives (Brock and Wangenheim, 2019).

Case Studies of Leadership Driving AI Initiatives Successfully

- **Amazon:** Jeff Bezos, the CEO of Amazon, has been a driving force behind the company's AI initiatives, particularly in the areas of customer service, logistics, and personalization. Under his leadership, Amazon has leveraged AI to optimize its supply chain, improve customer recommendations, and enhance its voice-activated assistant, Alexa. Bezos's focus on AI as a strategic priority has positioned Amazon as a leader in AI-driven business transformation (Yanamala, 2024).
- **Google:** Sundar Pichai, CEO of Google, has emphasized AI as central to the company's future growth. Google's leadership has integrated AI into every aspect of the company's operations, from search algorithms to cloud services. Pichai has promoted a culture of innovation and cross-functional collaboration, enabling Google to develop advanced AI tools that serve millions of users

worldwide. Google's success in AI can be attributed to Pichai's visionary leadership and his ability to align AI with the company's long-term goals (Hemphill, 2021).

- **Microsoft:** Under the leadership of Satya Nadella, Microsoft has become a leader in AI research and development. Nadella has positioned AI as a key component of Microsoft's cloud computing strategy, emphasizing AI-driven solutions for businesses across industries. His leadership has encouraged cross-functional collaboration and experimentation, leading to the development of innovative AI tools, such as Azure AI and Cortana. Nadella's commitment to AI innovation has helped Microsoft maintain its competitive edge in the tech industry (Schrettenbrunnner, 2020).

By adopting leadership strategies that emphasize vision, collaboration, and change management, these companies have successfully integrated AI into their operations and achieved significant competitive advantages.

CHALLENGES IN BUILDING AN AI-READY ORGANIZATION

Building an AI-ready organization presents several significant challenges that organizations must address to ensure the successful integration of AI technologies. These challenges are multifaceted and can stem from cultural, technical, and resource-related barriers. Additionally, AI-related fears, such as job displacement, ethical concerns, and transparency issues, can further complicate the process of AI adoption. This section discusses the common obstacles organizations face in becoming AI-ready, strategies for overcoming resistance, and the importance of fostering trust in AI technologies within the organization.

Common Obstacles in AI Readiness: Cultural, Technical, and Resource-related Challenges

The journey to becoming AI-ready is often hindered by a combination of internal and external factors. One of the most prominent barriers is the **cultural resistance** within organizations. Organizational culture plays a crucial role in determining how receptive employees are to AI integration. In many cases, employees may fear that AI will disrupt their job roles or eliminate certain positions altogether. According to Dhasarathy *et al.* (2020), organizations with rigid hierarchical structures or a lack of openness to innovation may struggle to adopt AI technologies.

Technical challenges are another significant obstacle. AI requires sophisticated infrastructure, including data storage capabilities, computing power, and technical expertise to develop and maintain AI systems. Organizations that lack the necessary technology stack or have limited access to data may find it difficult to deploy AI solutions effectively (Fenwick *et al.*, 2024). Additionally, organizations may struggle with integrating AI into legacy systems, which can create further roadblocks in AI adoption.

Resource-related challenges encompass both financial and human capital limitations. AI technologies can be expensive to implement, and not all organizations have the financial resources to invest in the necessary tools, platforms, and talent. Moreover, the shortage of skilled AI professionals creates additional challenges for organizations trying to build AI competency. The demand for data scientists, machine learning engineers, and AI specialists far exceeds the supply, making it difficult for organizations to attract and retain the talent needed for AI readiness (Polisetty *et al.*, 2024).

Addressing AI-related Fears: Job Displacement, Ethics, and Transparency

One of the most significant fears associated with AI adoption is the potential for job displacement. Employees may worry that AI will automate their roles, leading to widespread layoffs or the devaluation of human labor. According to a report by Tehrani *et al.* (2024), while AI is expected to create new job opportunities, there is still significant concern about the displacement of certain job functions, particularly in routine and manual tasks. To address these fears, organizations must emphasize the role of upskilling and reskilling. By offering training programs that equip employees with the necessary skills to work alongside AI technologies, organizations can mitigate concerns about job displacement and create a workforce that is capable of leveraging AI for more strategic tasks. Leaders must also communicate that AI is intended to augment human capabilities rather than replace them entirely, helping employees see AI as a tool for enhancing productivity and innovation (Ellefsen *et al.*, 2019).

Ethical concerns are another key issue in AI adoption. AI systems are often perceived as black boxes, where decision-making processes are opaque and difficult to understand. This lack of transparency can lead to fears of bias, discrimination, and unethical decision-making. For example, AI algorithms trained on biased datasets may inadvertently reinforce societal inequalities, leading to unfair outcomes in areas such as hiring, lending, and criminal justice (Daffner, 2024). To address these concerns, organizations must adopt responsible AI governance frameworks that promote fairness, accountability, and transparency in AI systems.

Strategies to Overcome Resistance to AI Integration

Overcoming resistance to AI integration requires a multifaceted approach. One effective strategy is to foster a culture of innovation and experimentation. By creating an environment where employees feel safe to test new ideas and embrace AI technologies, organizations can reduce resistance to change. Leaders must also be proactive in addressing employee concerns, engaging in open dialogues about the impact of AI on job roles, and involving employees in the decision-making process (Seidelson, 2021). Change management plays a critical role in overcoming resistance to AI adoption. Leaders should implement structured change management programs that guide employees through the transition to AI-enabled processes. This includes clear communication about the benefits of AI, providing training and resources to support AI adoption, and involving key stakeholders in the planning and execution of AI initiatives (Randriamiary, 2024). Organizations should also adopt pilot programs to demonstrate the value of AI before scaling its use across the organization. Pilot projects allow employees to see firsthand how AI can improve specific processes, such as decision-making, customer service, or operational efficiency. By showcasing tangible benefits, organizations can build employee buy-in and reduce skepticism about AI's role in the workplace.

Importance of Fostering Trust in AI Technologies Within the Organization

Building trust in AI technologies is essential for successful AI adoption. Employees must trust that AI systems are reliable, fair, and aligned with the organization's values. Trust can be fostered by ensuring that AI algorithms are transparent and explainable. Organizations should prioritize the development of interpretable AI models that provide clear insights into how decisions are made, allowing employees to understand and validate the outputs of AI systems (Upadhyay, 2023). Moreover, organizations must implement ethical AI frameworks that govern the use of AI technologies, ensuring that AI systems are free from bias and operate in a manner that is consistent with organizational values. This includes establishing ethical guidelines for data collection, algorithm development, and decision-making processes. By fostering a culture of ethical AI, organizations can build trust among employees, customers, and other stakeholders (Kidwai-Khan *et al.*, 2024).

The Role of Continuous Learning in AI-ready Organizations

As organizations integrate Artificial Intelligence (AI) into their business processes, the importance of continuous learning becomes critical. AI technologies evolve rapidly, and businesses must ensure that their employees are equipped with the skills and knowledge necessary to leverage these advancements. Continuous learning facilitates this by fostering an environment where employees can regularly update their skills and stay aligned with the evolving technological landscape.

Importance of Ongoing Education and Development in AI Adoption

The rapid pace of AI development means that knowledge and skills can quickly become outdated. Ongoing education is crucial for helping employees keep pace with new AI tools, algorithms, and applications. Continuous learning ensures that employees can effectively collaborate with AI systems, which in turn enhances the organization's ability to innovate and compete in an AI-driven marketplace. According to Aldoseri *et al.* (2024), organizations that invest in employee education and development can achieve higher levels of efficiency, adaptability, and innovation. A culture of learning also helps in overcoming the fear of automation, as employees feel empowered to work alongside AI rather than fearing job displacement. Additionally, continuous learning supports the long-term sustainability of AI adoption. Since AI is reshaping industries by automating repetitive tasks and offering predictive insights, employees must understand how to use these technologies to enhance decision-making and performance (Emanuel and Stone, 2024). Without adequate training, employees may resist AI integration, which can hinder organizational growth and digital transformation.

DESIGNING AI TRAINING PROGRAMS: AI LITERACY, DATA ANALYSIS, AND DIGITAL TOOLS

For organizations to become truly AI-ready, they must design comprehensive training programs that address various aspects of AI literacy. These programs should focus not only on the technical aspects of AI but also on enhancing employees' understanding of AI's implications for their roles and the organization as a whole.

- **AI Literacy:** A foundational component of AI training involves educating employees on basic AI concepts, including machine learning, automation, natural language processing, and predictive analytics. This helps employees understand the potential applications of AI in their work and across the business (Aldoseri *et al.*, 2024).
- **Data Analysis:** Since AI relies on data to generate insights and predictions, training programs must emphasize data literacy. Employees should learn how to work with large datasets, interpret AI-generated insights, and use data to inform business decisions (Emanuel and Stone, 2024). This is particularly important for roles that involve customer insights, market analysis, and strategic planning.
- **Digital Tools:** Organizations should also provide training on the specific AI tools and platforms they use. This includes cloud-based AI solutions, business intelligence platforms, and automation tools. By equipping employees with hands-on experience using AI tools, organizations can increase adoption rates and improve productivity (Henk and Nilssen, 2021).

Implementing Mentoring and Knowledge-sharing Platforms

To sustain continuous learning and ensure the long-term success of AI adoption, organizations should implement mentoring and knowledge-sharing platforms. Mentoring programs, where AI experts or external consultants guide less experienced employees, can accelerate learning and promote confidence in using AI tools. Knowledge-sharing platforms, such as online forums, intranet portals, or collaborative software tools, also encourage employees to share best practices, case studies, and innovative ideas related to AI usage. For example, companies like Google and Amazon have built extensive internal networks that allow employees to share AI-related knowledge, collaborate on AI projects, and receive mentorship from AI experts (Henk and Nilssen, 2021). This enables employees to continuously improve their skills and apply AI technologies more effectively to their work. Organizations should encourage cross-functional learning through these platforms, enabling employees from different departments to learn how AI can improve various aspects of the business. Interdepartmental knowledge sharing ensures that AI is adopted holistically across the organization and not confined to specific teams or functions.

ETHICAL AND GOVERNANCE ISSUES IN AI ADOPTION

As Artificial Intelligence (AI) becomes more pervasive in business operations, it raises important ethical and governance issues that organizations must address to ensure responsible and sustainable use of the technology. While AI has the potential to transform industries by optimizing decision-making and increasing efficiency, it also poses challenges related to bias, accountability, transparency, and data privacy. Ethical AI adoption is essential to maintain public trust, comply with regulations, and avoid unintended harm.

AI Ethics and Accountability in Decision-making

AI systems are increasingly used to automate decision-making processes in areas like hiring, customer service, credit scoring, and law enforcement. However, the ethical implications of these decisions need to be carefully considered, particularly when AI-driven decisions impact people's lives or livelihoods. AI systems can perpetuate or even exacerbate existing biases in data, leading to discriminatory outcomes. For instance, facial recognition algorithms have been shown to misidentify people of color at higher rates than others, raising concerns about fairness and justice in AI applications (Kankanhalli *et al.*, 2019). Organizations adopting AI must ensure accountability in decision-making. This involves identifying who is responsible when AI systems make flawed or harmful decisions. Traditional corporate governance structures may not be adequate to manage the unique challenges posed by AI, making it essential to develop new frameworks for accountability in AI-driven organizations (Cihon, 2019). Clear guidelines should define the roles of AI developers, data scientists, and business leaders in ensuring that AI decisions are ethically sound.

Governance Frameworks for Responsible AI Implementation

Implementing AI responsibly requires a robust governance framework that outlines policies and practices for managing AI systems throughout their lifecycle. These frameworks should address issues such as risk management, ethics, and compliance with regulations like the General Data Protection Regulation (GDPR). Organizations should establish governance bodies or ethics committees to oversee the development and deployment of AI technologies. A well-structured governance framework ensures that AI systems align with organizational values and public expectations. Google's AI Principles, for example, explicitly state that AI technologies should avoid causing harm, be built and tested for safety, and remain accountable to people (Taeihagh, 2021). Other organizations have followed suit by developing their own ethical guidelines for AI, focusing on principles such as fairness, transparency, and human oversight. Additionally, regulatory bodies are beginning to develop policies to govern AI. In the European Union, the Artificial Intelligence Act aims to regulate high-risk AI applications, such as those used in healthcare, transportation, and law enforcement, by requiring strict oversight, risk assessment, and accountability mechanisms. These governance frameworks help organizations navigate the ethical complexities of AI, ensuring that AI adoption is aligned with legal and societal expectations.

Managing Biases and Ensuring Transparency in AI Systems

AI systems rely heavily on data, and biases present in the training data can lead to biased AI outcomes. For example, if an AI system is trained on historical data that reflects societal inequalities, it can inadvertently perpetuate those inequalities. Bias in AI can manifest in various forms, including racial, gender, and socioeconomic biases, which can lead to discriminatory practices in hiring, lending, and law enforcement (Zuiderwijk *et al.*, 2021). To manage these biases, organizations need to adopt strategies for fairness and transparency in AI systems. This includes using diverse datasets that reflect a wide range of demographic groups and regularly auditing AI models to detect and mitigate biases. Algorithmic transparency is also crucial, as it allows stakeholders to understand how AI systems make decisions. Transparency builds trust in AI technologies by enabling users to scrutinize AI decisions and identify potential biases. Moreover, implementing explainability mechanisms in AI systems allows users to understand the reasoning behind AI-driven decisions, thus fostering greater accountability and user confidence.

Addressing Data Privacy and Security Concerns in an AI Context

One of the most critical governance issues in AI adoption is the protection of data privacy and security. AI systems often rely on vast amounts of personal data to train machine learning models, which can expose sensitive information to privacy risks. High-profile data breaches and misuse of personal data, such as the Cambridge Analytica scandal, have heightened public awareness and concerns about data privacy in AI applications (Lewis *et al.*, 2020). Organizations must ensure that they comply with data privacy regulations, such as the GDPR, which governs the collection, processing, and storage of personal data in the European Union (Schiff *et al.*, 2022). Data minimization practices, which involve collecting only the necessary data for a specific purpose, are essential in reducing privacy risks. Additionally, organizations should implement robust cybersecurity measures to protect sensitive data from unauthorized access and data breaches (Kamble, 2024). Moreover, AI systems should be designed with privacy by design principles, meaning that privacy considerations are integrated into the development process from the outset. Techniques like differential privacy and federated learning can enhance privacy protection by ensuring that AI models learn from data without directly accessing sensitive information (Sharma *et al.*, 2022).

FUTURE TRENDS IN AI-READY ORGANIZATIONS

Leadership in AI-driven enterprises is undergoing significant transformation. As AI becomes more integrated into strategic decision-making, leaders must adopt new leadership models that emphasize data-driven insights, agility, and innovation. Traditional top-down leadership styles are being replaced by more collaborative and decentralized models where decision-making is often supported by AI tools (Butcher and Beridze, 2019). AI-powered organizations require adaptive leaders who can understand AI's capabilities and limitations, foster a culture of continuous learning, and promote cross-functional collaboration. These leaders not only need to possess technological acumen but also the ability to manage change, inspire teams to embrace AI technologies and align AI initiatives with broader strategic goals (Ulnicane *et al.*, 2021). In the future, leaders will need to act as AI architects, guiding their organizations through complex AI integrations and ensuring that AI tools are aligned with human values and organizational objectives. Companies like IBM and Microsoft have already established leadership models where executives are responsible for steering AI development ethically while ensuring AI applications enhance overall business performance (RoskAttardi *et al.*, 2021).

The rise of AI is reshaping how organizations approach talent management. As AI takes on more operational and analytical roles, the skills required to thrive in an AI-driven enterprise are evolving. Talent management strategies must adapt to attract and retain individuals with specialized AI knowledge, such as data scientists, machine learning engineers, and AI ethicists (Truby, 2020). AI-ready organizations will need to implement robust talent acquisition and development strategies to build a workforce capable of driving AI innovation. This includes not only recruiting AI professionals but also upskilling and reskilling existing employees to work effectively with AI tools. Companies like Google and Amazon are at the forefront of this trend, offering extensive AI training programs and creating pathways for employees to gain AI competencies (Doya *et al.*, 2022). Moreover, AI-ready organizations will need to cultivate a culture of lifelong learning to remain competitive. In the future, AI training will likely become a cornerstone of professional development, and companies will increasingly invest in AI literacy programs to ensure that all employees, from entry-level workers to senior executives, understand AI's potential and applications (Elliott *et al.*, 2021).

The Growing Importance of Ethical AI Leadership

With the widespread adoption of AI, ethical leadership is becoming a critical component of successful AI-ready organizations. As AI systems become more involved in critical decision-making processes, leaders must prioritize ethical AI development to mitigate the risks of bias, discrimination, and transparency issues. Ethical AI leadership involves not only setting clear guidelines for responsible AI use but also ensuring that AI systems are designed and deployed in ways that reflect societal values and organizational integrity (Magomadov, 2020). In the future, ethical AI leadership will play a pivotal role in maintaining public trust and avoiding reputational damage. As AI technologies continue to evolve, so will the ethical dilemmas surrounding their use. Leaders will need to navigate complex ethical questions about data privacy, accountability, and the impact of AI on employment. Companies like Salesforce have already appointed Chief AI Ethics Officers to oversee the responsible deployment of AI technologies, signaling the growing importance of this leadership role (Hangl *et al.*, 2023).

Predictions on AI Integration in Organizational Structures

The integration of AI into organizational structures will continue to expand as AI technologies become more sophisticated and ubiquitous. In the future, AI is expected to take on a more prominent role in organizational decision-making, from daily operational decisions to long-term strategic planning. AI will increasingly automate routine tasks, allowing human workers to focus on more creative and complex problem-solving (Kuziemski and Misuraca, 2020).

Organizational structures are likely to evolve to accommodate AI-driven departments or units specifically focused on AI development and deployment. These departments will work closely with other business units, such as marketing, finance, and human resources, to ensure that AI is effectively integrated into all aspects of the organization (Carrillo, 2020). AI is also expected to reshape hierarchical models, as AI systems facilitate faster and more accurate decision-making at all levels of the organization, leading to flatter and more agile structures.

Cross-functional teams will become more common, with AI experts collaborating with business leaders to ensure that AI initiatives are aligned with overall business goals. Moreover, AI will enable more data-driven leadership as real-time data analysis becomes central to strategic decision-making. Organizations that successfully integrate AI into their structures will be better positioned to innovate, adapt to changing market conditions, and maintain a competitive edge in their industries (Smuha, 2021).

CONCLUSION

As organizations continue to navigate the complexities of integrating Artificial Intelligence (AI) into their operations, understanding the cultural, talent, and leadership dimensions of AI readiness has become paramount. This literature review highlights several key findings regarding the necessary components for fostering an AI-ready organization. The findings emphasize that organizational culture plays a critical role in facilitating AI adoption. A culture that promotes innovation, collaboration, and agility enables organizations to embrace AI technologies effectively. Companies that foster an AI-supportive environment can overcome cultural resistance and accelerate their AI integration efforts. Furthermore, the literature indicates that talent development is essential for AI readiness. Organizations must not only focus on acquiring new talent with AI expertise but also prioritize the upskilling and reskilling of existing employees to adapt to evolving technologies. The establishment of a learning culture that prioritizes continuous education is fundamental to maintaining competitiveness in the age of AI. Leadership also emerges as a pivotal element in building AI-ready organizations. Effective leaders must embrace visionary leadership that aligns AI initiatives with strategic business goals while fostering cross-functional collaboration. Ethical considerations in AI adoption highlight the need for leaders to prioritize responsible AI governance, ensuring that AI systems are implemented transparently and equitably.

Implications for Businesses Aiming to Build AI-ready Organizations

For businesses striving to become AI-ready, the implications of these findings are clear. Organizations should focus on cultivating a culture that encourages innovation and experimentation with AI technologies. This cultural shift may require dedicated change management initiatives to address any resistance and promote an understanding of AI's benefits. Additionally, businesses must invest in talent development strategies that encompass not only hiring practices but also robust training programs that equip employees with the necessary AI skills. By doing so, organizations can build a workforce capable of driving AI innovations and navigating the complexities of AI integration. Leadership plays a critical role in this transformation, as leaders must actively champion AI initiatives and create a clear vision for the organization's AI journey. Organizations should consider establishing governance frameworks that prioritize ethical AI practices and ensure accountability throughout the AI implementation process.

REFERENCES

Aldoseri, A., Al-Khalifa, K.N., Hamouda, A.M. (2024). AI-powered innovation in digital transformation: key pillars and industry impact. *Sustainability, 16*(5), 1790.
[http://dx.doi.org/10.3390/su16051790]

Allioui, H., Mourdi, Y. (2023). Unleashing the Potential of AI: Investigating cutting-edge technologies that are transforming businesses. *International Journal of Computer Engineering and Data Science, 3*(2), 2737-8543. Available from: https://ijceds.com/ijceds/article/view/59/25

Brock, J.K.U., von Wangenheim, F. (2019). Demystifying AI: What digital transformation leaders can teach you about realistic artificial intelligence. *California Management Review, 61*(4), 110-134.
[http://dx.doi.org/10.1177/1536504219865226]

Butcher, J., Beridze, I. (2019). What is the state of artificial intelligence governance globally? *RUSI Journal, 164*(5-6), 88-96.
[http://dx.doi.org/10.1080/03071847.2019.1694260]

Carrel, A. (2019). Legal intelligence through artificial intelligence requires emotional intelligence: a new competency model for the 21st century legal professional. *Georgia State University Law Review, 35*(4), 4. Available   from: https://readingroom.law.gsu.edu/gsulrAvailableat:https://readingroom.law.gsu.edu/gsulr/vol35/iss4/4

Castrounis, A. (2019). *AI for people and business: A framework for better human experiences and business success.*

Chen, H., Li, L., Chen, Y. (2021). Explore success factors that impact artificial intelligence adoption on telecom industry in China. *Journal of Management Analytics, 8*(1), 36-68.
[http://dx.doi.org/10.1080/23270012.2020.1852895]

Chowdhury, S., Dey, P., Joel-Edgar, S., Bhattacharya, S., Rodriguez-Espindola, O., Abadie, A., Truong, L. (2023). Unlocking the value of artificial intelligence in human resource management through AI capability framework. *Human Resource Management Review, 33*(1), 100899.
[http://dx.doi.org/10.1016/j.hrmr.2022.100899]

Cihon, P. (2019). Standards for AI Governance: International standards to enable global coordination in ai research & development. In future of humanity institute, University of Oxford (Issue April, pp. 1–41). .

Daffner, B. (2024). Are you AI-ready? A roadmap to mastering marketing technology in a data-driven world. *Journal of Digital & Social Media Marketing.12*(2), pp. 117-128, 2024. Available from: https://www.ingentaconnect.com/ content/hsp/jdsmm/2024/00000012/00000002/art00003.

Dhasarathy, A., Ghia, A., Griffiths, S., & Wavra, R. (2020). Accelerating AI impact by taming the data beast. In McKinsey (Issue March). Available from: https://www.mckinsey.com/industries/public-sector/our-

insights/accelerating-ai-impact-by-taming-the-data-beast?cid=other-eml-alt-mip-mck&hlkid=ffd1e6061a0
a4589ac0550926fc4cee1&hctky=11600154&hdpid=a26fa1fc-3987-4b75-8efd-1aca784aeb99.

Doya, K., Ema, A., Kitano, H., Sakagami, M., Russell, S. (2022). Social impact and governance of AI and neurotechnologies. *Neural Networks,* Elsevier.*152*, 542-554.
[http://dx.doi.org/10.1016/j.neunet.2022.05.012]

Ellefsen, A.P.T., Oleśków-Szłapka, J., Pawłowski, G., Toboła, A. (2019). Striving for excellence in AI implementation: AI maturity model framework and preliminary research results. *Logforum, 15*(3), 363-376.
[http://dx.doi.org/10.17270/J.LOG.2019.354]

Elliott, K., Price, R., Shaw, P., Spiliotopoulos, T., Ng, M., Coopamootoo, K., van Moorsel, A. (2021). Towards an equitable digital society: Artificial Intelligence (AI) and corporate digital responsibility (CDR). *Society, 58*(3), 179-188.
[http://dx.doi.org/10.1007/s12115-021-00594-8]

Emanuel, A., Stone, D. H. (2024). Exploring the profound impact of AI on higher education and students. *Academic Integrity in the Age of Artificial,* 112-138.
[http://dx.doi.org/10.4018/979-8-3693-0240-8.ch007]

Enholm, I.M., Papagiannidis, E., Mikalef, P., Krogstie, J. (2022). Artificial intelligence and business value: a literature review. *Information Systems Frontiers, 24*(5), 1709-1734.
[http://dx.doi.org/10.1007/s10796-021-10186-w]

Faqihi, A., Miah, S.J. (2023). Artificial intelligence-driven talent management system: exploring the risks and options for constructing a theoretical foundation. *Journal of Risk and Financial Management, 16*(1), 31.
[http://dx.doi.org/10.3390/jrfm16010031]

Fenwick, A., Molnar, G., Frangos, P. (2024). The critical role of HRM in AI-driven digital transformation: a paradigm shift to enable firms to move from AI implementation to human-centric adoption. *Discover Artificial Intelligence, 16*(4), 34.
[http://dx.doi.org/10.1007/s44163-024-00125-4]

Fountaine, T., McCarthy, B., & Saleh, T. (2019). Building the AI-powered organization. In *Harvard Business Review.* Available from: https://wuyuansheng.com/doc/Databricks-AI-Powered-Org__Article-Licensing-July21-1.pdf.

Füller, J., Hutter, K., Wahl, J., Bilgram, V., Tekic, Z. (2022). How AI revolutionizes innovation management – Perceptions and implementation preferences of AI-based innovators. *Technological Forecasting and Social Change.,* Elsevier.*178*, 121598.
[http://dx.doi.org/10.1016/j.techfore.2022.121598]

Hangl, J., Krause, S., Behrens, V.J. (2023). Drivers, barriers and social considerations for AI adoption in SCM. *Technology in Society, 74*, 102299.
[http://dx.doi.org/10.1016/j.techsoc.2023.102299]

Hansen, H.F., Lillesund, E., Mikalef, P., Altwaijry, N. (2024). Understanding Artificial Intelligence diffusion through an AI capability maturity model. *Information Systems Frontiers,* Springer.*26*, 2147-2163.
[http://dx.doi.org/10.1007/s10796-024-10528-4]

Hemphill, T. A. (2021). Book review: Competing in the Age of AI: Strategy and leadership when algorithms and networks run the world. In *Journal of General Management (Vol. 46,* Issue 4, pp. 322–323).
[http://dx.doi.org/10.1177/0306307020972520]

Henk, A., & Nilssen, F. (2021). Can AI become a state servant? A case study of an intelligent chatbot implementation in a scandinavian public service. In Proceedings of the Annual Hawaii International Conference on System Sciences (Vols. 2020-January). Available from: scholarspace.manoa.hawaii.edu.
[http://dx.doi.org/10.24251/HICSS.2021.670]

Jöhnhrabei, J., Weißert, M., Wyrtki, K. (2021). Ready or Not, AI comes— an interview study of organizational ai readiness factors. *Business and Information Systems Engineering, 63*(1), 5-20.
[http://dx.doi.org/10.1007/s12599-020-00676-7]

Kamble, R.M. (2024). Artificial intelligence and human rights. *Uniform Law Review, 29*(1), 77-86. [http://dx.doi.org/10.1093/ulr/unae020]

Kankanhalli, A., Charalabidis, Y., Mellouli, S. (2019). IoT and AI for smart government: A research agenda. *Government Information Quarterly, 36*(2), 304-309. [http://dx.doi.org/10.1016/j.giq.2019.02.003]

Kidwai-Khan, F., Wang, R., Skanderson, M., Brandt, C.A., Fodeh, S., Womack, J.A. (2024). A roadmap to artificial intelligence (AI): Methods for designing and building AI ready data to promote fairness. *Journal of Biomedical Informatics, 154*, 104654. [http://dx.doi.org/10.1016/j.jbi.2024.104654] [PMID: 38740316]

Kulkov, I., Kulkova, J., Rohrbeck, R., Menvielle, L., Kaartemo, V., Makkonen, H. (2024). Artificial intelligence - driven sustainable development: Examining organizational, technical, and processing approaches to achieving global goals. *Sustainable Development, 32*(3), 2253-2267. [http://dx.doi.org/10.1002/sd.2773]

Kuziemski, M., Misuraca, G. (2020). AI governance in the public sector: Three tales from the frontiers of automated decision-making in democratic settings. *Telecommunications Policy, 44*(6), 101976. [http://dx.doi.org/10.1016/j.telpol.2020.101976] [PMID: 32313360]

Lewis, D., Hogan, L., Filip, D., Wall, P.J. (2020). Global challenges in the standardization of ethics for trustworthy AI. *Journal of ICT Standardization, 8*(2), 123-150. [http://dx.doi.org/10.13052/jicts2245-800X.823]

Lilly, A., Rajkumar, R., Amudha, R. (2022). Aggrandizing the human resource development with underpinning artificial intelligence. *Journal of Statistics and Management Systems, 25*(5), 1083-1094. [http://dx.doi.org/10.1080/09720510.2022.2040859]

Magomadov, V.S. (2020). The application of artificial intelligence in radiology. *Journal of Physics: Conference Series, 1515*(5), 052062. [http://dx.doi.org/10.1088/1742-6596/1515/5/052062]

Malik, A., De Silva, M.T.T., Budhwar, P., Srikanth, N.R. (2021). Elevating talents' experience through innovative artificial intelligence-mediated knowledge sharing: Evidence from an IT-multinational enterprise. *Journal of International Management, 27*(4), 100871. [http://dx.doi.org/10.1016/j.intman.2021.100871]

Mikalef, P., Gupta, M. (2021). Artificial intelligence capability: Conceptualization, measurement calibration, and empirical study on its impact on organizational creativity and firm performance. *Information and Management, 58*(3). [http://dx.doi.org/10.1016/j.im.2021.103434]

Mishra, R., Rodriguez, R., & Portillo, V. (2020). An AI based talent acquisition and benchmarking for job. ArXiv Preprint ArXiv:2009.09088. http://arxiv.org/abs/2009.09088.

Odugbesan, J.A., Aghazadeh, S., Al Qaralleh, R.E., Sogeke, O.S. (2023). Green talent management and employees' innovative work behavior: the roles of artificial intelligence and transformational leadership. *Journal of Knowledge Management, 27*(3), 696-716. [http://dx.doi.org/10.1108/JKM-08-2021-0601]

Ogbeibu, S., Chiappetta Jabbour, C.J., Burgess, J., Gaskin, J., Renwick, D.W.S. (2022). Green talent management and turnover intention: the roles of leader STARA competence and digital task interdependence. *Journal of Intellectual Capital, 23*(1), 27-55. [http://dx.doi.org/10.1108/JIC-01-2021-0016]

Paramita, D. (2020). Digitalization in Talent Acquisition: A Case Study of AI in Recruitment. In Samint-Mili Nv - 20035: Vol. Independen (Issue June). Available from: http://uu.diva-portal.org/smash/get/diva2:1440107/FULLTEXT01.pdf%0Ahttp://urn.kb.se/resolve?urn=urn:nbn:se:uu:diva-413081.

Pathak, S., Solanki, V.K. (2021). Impact of internet of things and artificial intelligence on human resource development. In: Balas, VE, Solanki, VK and Kumar, R (Eds). *Further Advances in Internet of Things in*

Biomedical and Cyber Physical Systems, .193, 239-267.
[http://dx.doi.org/10.1007/978-3-030-57835-0_19]

Pillai, R., Sivathanu, B. (2020). Adoption of AI-based chatbots for hospitality and tourism. *International Journal of Contemporary Hospitality Management, 32*(10), 3199-3226. a
[http://dx.doi.org/10.1108/IJCHM-04-2020-0259]

Pillai, R., Sivathanu, B. (2020). Adoption of artificial intelligence (AI) for talent acquisition in IT/ITeS organizations. *Benchmarking (Bradf.), 27*(9), 2599-2629. b
[http://dx.doi.org/10.1108/BIJ-04-2020-0186]

Polisetty, A., Chakraborty, D., G, S., Kar, A.K., Pahari, S. (2024). What Determines AI Adoption in Companies? Mixed-Method Evidence. *Journal of Computer Information Systems, 64*(3), 370-387.
[http://dx.doi.org/10.1080/08874417.2023.2219668]

Randriamiary, D. (2024). Reframing the role of leaders navigating the challenges and opportunities of tomorrow's workplace in the age of Artificial Intelligence. *SSRN,* 4716033.
[http://dx.doi.org/10.2139/ssrn.4716033]

Rožman, M., Oreški, D., Tominc, P. (2022). Integrating artificial intelligence into a talent management model to increase the work engagement and performance of enterprises. *Frontiers in Psychology, 3.*
[http://dx.doi.org/10.3389/fpsyg.2022.1014434]

Schiff, D., Biddle, J., Borenstein, J., Laas, K. (2020). What's next for AI ethics, policy, and governance? A global overview. *AIES 2020 - Proceedings of the AAAI/ACM Conference on AI, Ethics, and Society,* 153-158.
[http://dx.doi.org/10.1145/3375627.3375804]

Schiff, D.S., Schiff, K.J., Pierson, P. (2022). Assessing public value failure in government adoption of artificial intelligence. *Public Administration, 100*(3), 653-673.
[http://dx.doi.org/10.1111/padm.12742]

Schrettenbrunnner, M. B. (2020). Artificial-intelligence-driven management. *IEEE Engineering Management.* Available from: https://ieeexplore.ieee.org/abstract/document/9079641/.

Seidelson, C.E. (2021). Is Artificial Intelligence (A.I.) Ready to run a factory? *Journal on Engineering, Science and Technology,* 126-132. Available from: pdfs.semanticscholar.org
[http://dx.doi.org/10.46328/ijonest.52]

Sharma, H., Soetan, T., Farinloye, T., Mogaji, E., Noite, M. D. F. (2022). AI adoption in universities in emerging economies: prospects, challenges and recommendations. In: Mogaji, E, Jain, V, Maringe, F and Hinson, RE (Eds) *Re-Imagining Educational Futures in Developing Countries: Lessons from Global Health Crises,,* 159-174.
[http://dx.doi.org/10.1007/978-3-030-88234-1_9]

Shen, G. (2022). AI-enabled talent training for the cross-cultural news communication talent. *Technological Forecasting and Social Change, 185*, 122031.
[http://dx.doi.org/10.1016/j.techfore.2022.122031]

Shrestha, Y.R., Ben-Menahem, S.M., von Krogh, G. (2019). Organizational decision-making structures in the age of Artificial Intelligence. *California Management Review, 61*(4), 66-83.
[http://dx.doi.org/10.1177/0008125619862257]

Smuha, N.A. (2021). From a 'race to AI' to a 'race to AI regulation': regulatory competition for artificial intelligence. *Law, Innovation and Technology, 13*(1), 57-84.
[http://dx.doi.org/10.1080/17579961.2021.1898300]

Taeihagh, A. (2021). Governance of artificial intelligence. *Policy and Society, 40*(2), 137-157.
[http://dx.doi.org/10.1080/14494035.2021.1928377]

Tehrani, A.N., Ray, S., Roy, S.K., Gruner, R.L., Appio, F.P. (2024). Decoding AI readiness: An in-depth analysis of key dimensions in multinational corporations. *Technovation, 131*, 102948.

[http://dx.doi.org/10.1016/j.technovation.2023.102948]

Truby, J. (2020). Governing Artificial Intelligence to benefit the UN sustainable development goals. *Sustainable Development, 28*(4), 946-959.
[http://dx.doi.org/10.1002/sd.2048]

Ulnicane, I., Knight, W., Leach, T., Stahl, B.C., Wanjiku, W.G. (2021). Framing governance for a contested emerging technology: Insights from AI policy. *Policy and Society, 40*(2), 158-177.
[http://dx.doi.org/10.1080/14494035.2020.1855800]

Upadhyay, D. (2023). How Does AI pose challenges for leaders in organizations? - a conceptual study. *Journal of Educational & Psychological Research, 5*(3), 720-727.
[http://dx.doi.org/10.33140/JEPR.05.03.03]

Venkatesh, V. (2022). Adoption and use of AI tools: A research agenda grounded in UTAUT. *Annals of Operations Research, 308*(1-2), 641-652.
[http://dx.doi.org/10.1007/s10479-020-03918-9]

Wang, X., Li, L., Tan, S.C., Yang, L., Lei, J. (2023). Preparing for AI-enhanced education: Conceptualizing and empirically examining teachers' AI readiness. *Computers in Human Behavior, 146*, 107798.
[http://dx.doi.org/10.1016/j.chb.2023.107798]

Whitlock, C., Strickland, F. (2022). The three imperatives to develop AI leaders. *Winning the National Security AI Competition: A Practical Guide for Government and Industry Leaders.* (pp. 1-11). Berkeley, CA: Apress.

Yanamala, K. K. R. (2024). Strategic implications of AI integration in workforce planning and talent forecasting. *Journal of Advanced Computing Systems.* Available from: https://scipublication.com/index.php/JACS/article/view/28.

Zuiderwijk, A., Chen, Y.C., Salem, F. (2021). Implications of the use of artificial intelligence in public governance: A systematic literature review and a research agenda. *Government Information Quarterly, 38*(3), 101577.
[http://dx.doi.org/10.1016/j.giq.2021.101577]

CHAPTER 3

Ethical Considerations in AI-driven Business Strategies

Abstract: This chapter explores the ethical considerations integral to AI-driven business strategies, emphasizing how fairness, transparency, accountability, and data privacy shape the responsible use of AI. The findings indicate that ethical AI integration is crucial for maintaining organizational integrity, public trust, and social welfare. Businesses must adhere to principles of fairness, accountability, transparency, and data privacy to prevent reputational damage, operational risks, and stakeholder distrust. AI applications that propagate biases compromise privacy, or lack proper oversight can lead to significant ethical and strategic challenges. The research underscores the importance of leadership in fostering ethical AI use, advocating for structured oversight mechanisms, ethical governance frameworks, and transparency tools such as explainable AI. Additionally, businesses must actively engage in inclusive data practices, conduct accountability audits, and stay informed about emerging regulations to mitigate ethical risks.

Keywords: AI-driven business, Algorithms, Ethical, Ethical framework, Policy development.

INTRODUCTION

AI-integrated business strategies have improved efficiency, personalization, and innovation. AI's ability to process massive datasets, predict trends, and support data-driven decisions has given businesses an unprecedented advantage in adapting to fast-changing markets and customer demands (Ahmad, 2024). Responsible AI use requires ethical considerations as AI transforms businesses. Beyond operational risks, ethical issues affect society, individuals, and organizations. Ethical AI practises must address bias, fairness, accountability, transparency, and data privacy to build trust and benefit all stakeholders (Aldoseri *et al.*, 2023). AI-driven decisions affect consumers, workers, and society, complicating fairness and bias. AI can discriminate in lending, healthcare, and hiring due to biased data or algorithms. Historical biases in neutral algorithm training data can perpetuate inequality (Nassar and Kamal, 2021). These biases worsen social and economic disparities and harm people and organizations, making them a top AI ethical concern. To ensure fairness and ethics, algorithms must be designed, tested, and monitored for bias as AI becomes more embedded in decision-making (Walz and Firth-Butterfield, 2019).

AI business ethics require data security and privacy. As data collection grows, businesses gain massive access to sensitive consumer and employee data. Under GDPR and CCPA, businesses must obtain clear consent, ensure data accuracy, and protect user rights to access and control personal data (Yaseen, 2022). These regulations emphasize ethical AI practices that prioritize personal data privacy and security to meet evolving privacy standards and consumer expectations. As AI applications evolve, businesses must be transparent about data usage, secure data, and follow privacy laws to avoid legal issues and build consumer trust (Yaseen, 2023).

Another ethical issue is the AI system and organisation accountability (Schiff *et al.*, 2020). AI accountability is crucial as business-oriented AI decisions increase. AI-driven decisions that directly affect people in healthcare, finance, and law enforcement require accountability mechanisms to establish clear ownership of decisions and outcomes (Zarifis *et al.*, 2023). Communicating AI system decisions builds stakeholder trust and intervention. To ensure transparency and accountability in AI systems, businesses should develop auditable, interpretable models for technical and non-technical stakeholders (Tomičić and Mosler, 2022). Integrating ethical AI into business processes requires governance. Leaders and decision-making authorities must promote social and organizational ethics. Ethical guidelines, interdisciplinary ethics committees, and AI training help companies adopt ethical AI (Klimova *et al.*, 2023). Businesses can deploy responsible AI with the IEEE and EU's recent AI ethics frameworks' fairness, accountability, and transparency principles (Roche *et al.*, 2023). Leadership and careful planning are needed to implement these frameworks for industry needs (Egorenkov, 2024).

AI's ethical implications grow as businesses adopt it. Ethics complicate AI use in organizations. Business AI ethics ensure fair, accountable, and transparent AI use. This literature review will explain AI ethics, AI deployment, and goals. A comprehensive analysis should show how ethical AI practices affect business strategies. Many AI ethics rules govern responsible AI technology use. AI ethics considers algorithm biases, transparency, and accountability (Ahmad, 2024). AI ethics reduce discrimination, privacy breaches, and other issues. Social inequality data can train machine learning algorithms to reinforce biases. These biases must be addressed to make AI systems fair and avoid stereotypes (Aldoseri *et al.*, 2023).

Data-driven companies are affected by AI ethics. As technology's ethical implications become clearer, consumers demand business transparency and accountability. Companies must navigate a complex ethical landscape to gain credibility. Ethical AI failures can damage law, reputation, and customer loyalty (Nassar and Kamal, 2021). Cambridge Analytica was criticized and regulated for unethical data use (Walz and Firth-Butterfield, 2019). Therefore, ethical AI deployment helps companies innovate responsibly and grow sustainably (Yaseen, 2022). Ethics are required for current and future AI regulations. Global governments and regulators are developing AI ethics guidelines. The EU's AI ethics regulations emphasise transparency, accountability, and human oversight (Yaseen, 2023). Ethical AI frameworks help companies comply with regulations and gain a competitive edge by being responsible corporate citizens.

This literature review defines AI ethics and synthesizes business AI ethics research to identify gaps and suggest future research. This chapter discusses ethical AI deployment practices, ethical AI framework implementation challenges, and ways to improve AI-driven business strategies' ethical considerations. This chapter helps practitioners and scholars by analyzing AI and ethical business practices. Organisations struggle with AI deployment ethics. Industry adoption of IEEE and EU AI ethics is low (Zarifis *et al.*, 2023). Businesses responsible for AI implementation may be confused by a lack of ethics. Conflicts between ethical and business objectives can arise when organizations struggle to balance innovation and ethical oversight (Tomičić and Mosler, 2022). Ethics matter as AI is integrated into business strategies. Modern companies must understand AI deployment ethics. Ethics builds stakeholder trust, reduces risks, and positions companies for long-term success. This literature review promotes business AI ethics and responsible AI adoption.

This chapter covered the ethical implications of AI in business strategy and its opportunities and responsibilities. The first section examined key ethical frameworks and guidelines and then examined AI-driven decision-making ethical issues like bias, accountability, and data privacy. The chapter also discusses sector-specific ethical dilemmas using examples from industries where AI has transformed operations and introduced complex ethical issues. The chapter also stressed transparency and data responsibility, suggesting best practices for organizations to address AI's unique ethical challenges. It concluded with an examination of regulatory and technological changes that will shape AI-driven business strategies' ethical landscape. This chapter helped practitioners and scholars ethically apply AI in business by analyzing real-world case studies and industry applications. The chapter sought to explain how AI could be used for competitive advantage in accordance with the ethical values necessary for sustainable business practices in a data-driven era.

LITERATURE REVIEW

Ethical Frameworks and Guidelines for AI

As AI changes industries and business practices, strong ethical guidelines are needed. These frameworks address AI deployment's ethical implications to ensure organizations follow society's rules. IEEE and EU standards are necessary for ethical AI. This section will cover these frameworks and fundamental principles like fairness, transparency, accountability, and companies creating AI ethical guidelines. Technology standards organization IEEE promotes AI ethics through "Ethically Aligned Design". This initiative sets AI system design human rights and ethics guidelines (Alam, 2023). Trustworthy AI guidelines from the European Commission emphasize accountability, transparency, and data governance (Jobin *et al*., 2019). These guidelines promote legal, ethical, and technically sound AI systems for society.

AI ethics relies on fundamentals. Fairness eliminates biases that can cause discrimination and unjust AI decisions (Nassar and Kamal, 2021). By making AI systems understandable, transparency builds trust. Organizational accountability for AI system decisions builds stakeholder trust and reduces AI deployment risks. Organizations must integrate ethical principles into AI initiatives to ensure responsible systems that uphold human rights and social norms (Cartolovni and Tomičić, 2022). Companies must develop AI ethical guidelines in addition to frameworks. The company must promote responsible AI use and ethical decision-making at all levels (Mittelstadt, 2019). Employees can use internal ethical guidelines to create and implement AI technologies that reflect the company's values. Ethics-promoting companies reduce AI risks and improve stakeholder trust and reputation (Shneiderman, 2020).

AI ethics can improve with industry standards. AI medical decision-making must protect patient privacy and welfare (Weber-Lewerenz, 2021). Financial industry algorithmic decision-making transparency and fairness govern credit scoring and lending (Peters *et al*., 2020). Industrial guidelines supplement ethical frameworks with sector-specific guidance. Companies develop and follow ethics. Companies must assess AI project ethics as technology advances. Organisational ethics mitigate AI deployment risks and ensure social compliance (Schiff *et al*., 2020). In a conscientious market where consumers expect technology transparency and accountability, ethical AI companies are more likely to succeed. Organisations must develop and follow AI ethics to use AI responsibly. IEEE and EU frameworks govern ethical AI, while organizations prioritize fairness, transparency, and accountability. Promoting ethics and responsible innovation, and creating internal ethical guidelines, can help companies navigate AI ethics. AI projects that follow these guidelines improve ethics and society, as shown in Fig. (**1**).

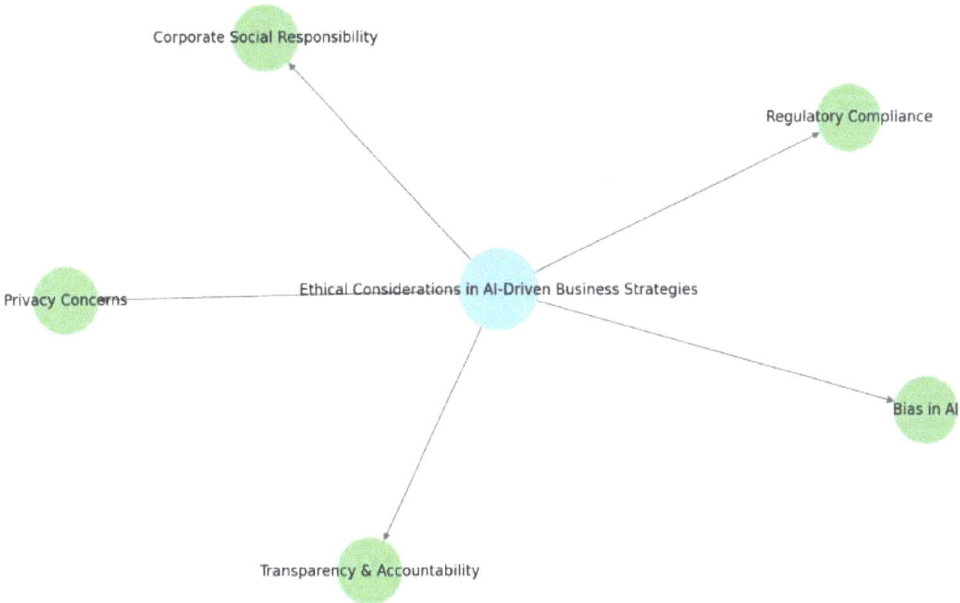

Fig. (1). Conceptual framework.

Bias and Discrimination in AI Systems

Poorly designed algorithms and biased data can cause AI to be biased. Data-related bias reinforces stereotypes when AI model datasets reflect historical inequalities or incomplete representations. Historical data from a male-dominated workforce may perpetuate gender bias in hiring algorithms (Giovanola and Tiribelli, 2023). Predictive policing algorithms trained in heavily policed neighborhoods may target minorities (Cirillo *et al.*, 2020). However, algorithmic bias occurs when model design or assumptions favor certain outcomes. Representative data can be biased. Facial recognition software algorithm or design changes can widen demographic accuracy gaps. Facial recognition algorithms make more mistakes for women and people of color due to biased training and a lack of diversity testing (Roselli *et al.*, 2019).

Case Studies Illustrating the Impact of Bias on Decision-Making

Multiple industry case studies show how bias affects decision-making, which leads to social and ethical issues. MIT researchers found that major tech companies' facial recognition algorithms misidentified darker-skinned women more than men. Legal issues and wrongful arrests can result from facial recognition software bias in law enforcement applications, disproportionately affecting marginalized groups (Varona and Suárez, 2022). AI-based healthcare resource allocation for poor Black patients. Ntoutsi *et al.* (2020) found that using healthcare cost data rather than health needs biased the algorithm that prioritized patients for additional care. Due to lower historical healthcare expenditures, the algorithm underestimated black patients' needs and reduced their likelihood of receiving additional care. Data selection biases affect health outcomes in this case study. AI hiring tool at Amazon degraded women's resumes, showing bias. This bias was caused by training the model on 10-year-old male-dominated company resumes. Instead of impartial selection, the algorithm exacerbated gender biases (Curto *et al.*, 2024).

Strategies for Mitigating Bias in AI

Combating AI bias requires inclusion, model evaluation, and algorithmic transparency. Demographically diverse data works. Training data with diverse samples balances race, gender, age, and socioeconomic status to reduce bias (Wellner and Rothman, 2020). Racial and gender biases can be reduced by training facial recognition datasets with different skin tones, facial structures, and expressions. Monitoring and assessing AI models is another option. To identify and address biases, AI models must be tested regularly as data and environments change. Before scaling, adversarial testing shows biases in AI systems through diverse edge cases (Silberman *et al.*, 2020). Audits and fairness checks reduce unintended discrimination by ensuring algorithm fairness across user groups. Communicate to reduce bias. Making AI systems more interpretable helps developers and users spot bias and decision-making. Model tools reveal biased correlations and algorithm attributes that affect decision-making. LIME and SHAP identify AI model outcomes-affecting features for fairer decision-making (Serna *et al.*, 2022). Ethics and operations like AI bias and discrimination need proactive solutions. Through bias analysis, case studies, and mitigation, organizations can improve AI systems. Inclusive data, transparent algorithmic design, and regular AI model evaluation are needed to eliminate bias and ensure ethical AI-driven decision-making.

Accountability and Transparency in AI Decision-Making

Accountability and transparency are crucial for AI business systems, which make decisions impacting consumers, employees, and regulators. To maintain trust, fairness, and ethics, AI-based decision-making must be accountable and transparent (Angerschmid *et al.*, 2022). AI-driven decision accountability, AI transparency mechanisms, and successful transparency practices are to be covered in this chapter. AI system accountability refers to the responsibility for decisions and actions made by AI models. This also encompasses business accountability for any AI-related errors, biases, or harm. However, the complex algorithms and datasets that underpin AI models can often obscure this accountability.Ingrams *et al.* (2022) recommend strong accountability frameworks for AI decision-making risks in high-stakes industries like finance, healthcare, and criminal justice.

The "black box" problem makes AI algorithms, especially deep learning models, hard to understand, complicating AI accountability. According to a study, complex AI outcomes complicate accountability as well (Lucic *et al.*, 2022). Therefore, businesses must establish clear accountability structures, including roles for monitoring AI outcomes and internal policies for addressing AI-driven errors or biases. AI models must be understandable for stakeholders to decide. Explainable AI (XAI) improves AI system comprehension without affecting performance, making it essential for transparency. LIME and SHAP boost stakeholder trust and AI prediction transparency by revealing feature contributions (Nassar and Kamal, 2021).

Systematic AI system evaluations and auditability increase transparency. AI inputs, results, and algorithms are bias- and risk-tested. Audits ensure AI systems meet internal and regulatory standards, increasing transparency and accountability. Transparency is increased by reporting AI models and decision processes with "model cards," which include data sources, performance metrics, and biases or limitations (Kim *et al.*, 2020). This helps stakeholders evaluate AI model strengths and weaknesses, improving AI-driven decisions. Businesses make crucial decisions with AI, so ethical AI deployment requires accountability and transparency. XAI and auditability make AI fair and accountable. Transparent companies build stakeholder trust and reduce risks. Transparent AI by Google, JPMorgan Chase, and IBM Watson Health promotes ethics. Responsibility and transparency are needed for responsible and equitable AI applications in diverse industries as AI becomes more important in business strategies.

Data Privacy and Security Concerns

Ethical AI deployment requires data privacy and security because AI systems use lots of personal data. To protect user privacy and security, organizations must address regulatory, ethical, and operational issues as AI-powered systems analyze and draw conclusions from data. The 2018 GDPR requires user consent, data minimization, and the right to be forgotten for data collection, storage, and processing. These regulations mandate privacy-by-design AI systems, which greatly impact AI development and use (Frik *et al.*, 2019). To protect rights and transparency, AI systems that handle personal data must protect privacy during design and operation.

The CCPA lets CA residents see and opt out of data sales. This law affects AI applications that train or predict using abundant and sensitive consumer data in retail, finance, and healthcare (Gallardo *et al.*, 2023). The GDPR and CCPA require AI companies to anonymize and give users data control. AI collects, stores, and uses massive amounts of personal data, raising ethical concerns. Data misuse, privacy violations, and public distrust can result from unethical data practices. Data reuse without consent risks exploitation and privacy loss, a major ethical issue. Targeted advertising using customer support data without consent may violate privacy and trust (Ioannou *et al.*, 2020).

Data storage and security are crucial. AI must prevent data breaches and internal access that leak sensitive data. Companies should store only necessary data and protect users' privacy with AI model training data (Rohunen and Markkula, 2019). This reduces data exposure and abuse and promotes ethical AI-driven business data handling. Data security is needed for regulations, privacy, and AI application integrity.

Data anonymization, encryption, and differential privacy are AI security best practices. Encrypting data storage and transmission protects sensitive data. Anonymised data allows modelling and analysis without identifying individuals (Kunduru, 2023). Datasets with differential privacy add noise by analyzing sensitive data without revealing it. This method gives large AI training organisations data insights while protecting privacy and reducing identity leakage (Pratama *et al.*, 2022). Strong audit trails allow organizations to restrict data access to authorized personnel and track data handling throughout its lifecycle. This method reduces data misuse and exposure while complying with ethics and law.

Data governance and security audits aid AI-driven decision-makers. Security audits find AI system vulnerabilities, protecting data quickly. ISO/IEC 27001 standardizes risk assessment, access control, and incident response (Lee and Ahmed, 2021). These practices encourage ethical AI data use and business data sustainability. GDPR and CCPA regulate data privacy and security for ethical AI-driven businesses. Organizations must address ethical data collection, storage, and use to protect user privacy and reduce misuse. Data security, trust, and regulatory compliance improve with encryption, anonymization, and differential privacy. Moral data privacy and security will help companies protect users' rights and adapt to changing legal and ethical standards as AI changes business strategies.

ETHICAL IMPLICATIONS OF AI IN SPECIFIC INDUSTRIES

When AI spreads across sectors, its ethical implications become more nuanced and context-specific. Industries have different ethical issues based on operations, regulations, and data. AI in healthcare raises ethical concerns because it directly affects patient health and privacy. Data privacy, consent, and security are concerns that arise when AI models are trained on PHI for diagnosis, treatment, and patient monitoring (Abulibdeh *et al.*, 2024). Insufficient demographic diversity in historical data may lead AI algorithms to treat underrepresented populations unfairly (Chan, 2023). Complex algorithm opacity can also make AI-assisted medical decision transparency and accountability controversial among patients and practitioners.

Finance ethics involve fairness, transparency, and accountability. Financial institutions use AI for credit scoring, loan approvals, and investment advice. Finance AI models trained on biased datasets can reinforce social and economic biases (Hagerty and Rubinov, 2019). A credit scoring algorithm that learns from past lending decisions may penalize certain demographic groups if historical data shows discriminatory lending. Financial transparency is another issue because algorithmic decision-making can make it hard for customers to understand why they were denied credit, eroding trust and accountability.

Marketing ethical issues include data privacy and manipulation. AI-driven advertising platforms use consumer data to personalise marketing campaigns, raising consent and data usage concerns (Jobin *et al.*, 2019). Using behavioral data, these AI systems can predict consumer preferences and exploit consumer vulnerabilities with intrusive or manipulative marketing. Ethical debates surround "dark patterns," or design tactics that steer users toward unwise choices, and AI's role in consumer behavior (Kaplan and Haenlein, 2019).

Case Studies Highlighting Ethical Dilemmas and Solutions Across Different Sectors

Several case studies show how these industries handle ethics. A major hospital's AI-driven diagnostic tool raised data transparency and informed consent concerns. Patients worried about the tool's lack of transparency because they didn't know the data used to make recommendations (Kerr *et al.*, 2020). In response, the hospital added informed consent layers to allow patients to opt out of AI-driven diagnostics. An AI-driven credit assessment tool hurt certain financial groups. After criticism, the bank updated the model's training data and added bias audits. Customers received transparent AI decision updates, promoting accountability (Rességuier and Rodrigues, 2020). AI-driven social media ad targeting was criticized for using personal data without consent to deliver highly personalized ads based on sensitive user behavior. After public backlash, the company tightened data protection policies, requiring user consent for certain data usage and giving users more data sharing control. Transparency restored user trust and showed ethical AI-driven marketing personalization (Mittelstadt, 2019).

Best Practices for Maintaining Ethical AI Standards in these Sectors

AI ethics can be navigated by industries using best practices that meet their operational and ethical needs. Explainable AI (XAI) tools should be used in healthcare to make AI-generated recommendations transparent for doctors and patients (Weber-Lewerenz, 2021). A diverse dataset that represents a variety of demographics can help healthcare AI reduce bias and treat all patients fairly, addressing ethical concerns. Continuous monitoring and auditing of finance AI models helps identify and correct biases early in decision-making. AI algorithms with fairness constraints can help financial institutions treat demographic groups equally (Wirtz *et al.*, 2019). By explaining credit or investment decisions to consumers, explainable AI frameworks build trust between financial institutions and their clients. Data governance policies that prioritize user consent and privacy are essential for ethical AI marketing. Marketing companies should disclose data personalization and allow opt-outs (Breidbach and Maglio, 2020). AI ethics that discourage manipulation can help marketers ensure AI-driven marketing respects consumer autonomy and does not exploit user vulnerabilities. As AI grows, companies must consider ethics. Businesses can use AI ethically and build stakeholder trust by learning from sector-specific ethical dilemmas and implementing best practices. Consider transparency, accountability, and fairness when navigating AI ethics to benefit society without compromising industry ethics.

The Role of Leadership in Ethical AI Adoption

Leaders structure an organization's ethics and create ethical AI policies that meet organizational and regulatory requirements. Ethics like fairness, transparency, and accountability must be discussed in AI development teams (Braganza *et al.*, 2021). Publicly promoting ethical AI shows leaders' commitment to responsible innovation, which can build brand trust with customers, employees, and stakeholders (Campion *et al.*, 2022). AI framework and policy development must be overseen by leaders. Set data privacy, bias, and transparency standards and hold employees accountable. Leaders must also foster this culture of ethics. This requires leading by example, prioritising ethical AI use, and ingraining these values in the organisation (Daly *et al.*, 2019).

Strategies for Encouraging Ethical AI Practices

Leadership can promote ethical AI practices in their organizations in several ways. They can start with comprehensive employee AI ethics training. The programs should teach employees how to use AI responsibly by covering bias detection, data usage, and privacy. Leaders can update their teams on AI ethics by providing ongoing training (Hasija and Esper, 2022). Ethical AI also requires policymaking. Leaders should work with data scientists, lawyers, and ethicists on AI development and deployment policies. The policies must include algorithm design fairness, data handling standards, and accountability. Explainable AI (XAI) and regular audits can help leaders disclose AI decision-making to internal teams and external stakeholders (Jobin *et al.*, 2019). A moral AI culture requires accountability. Leaders should establish clear reporting and ethical compliance review mechanisms to hold teams accountable. Periodic bias and fairness assessments of AI models can ensure ethical compliance. Open communication allows leaders to encourage employees to raise ethical concerns without fear of repercussions, creating an environment where ethical issues are proactively addressed rather than hidden (Nassar and Kamal, 2021).

Case Studies of Leadership-driven Ethical AI Transformations

Several organizations demonstrate how leadership affects ethical AI adoption. IBM leadership promotes AI transparency and trust. To explain AI decision-making to users and stakeholders, IBM leaders have promoted transparency. The IBM AI Ethics Board promotes AI ethics and transparency (Taeihagh, 2021). Leadership again drives Microsoft's ethical AI transformation. Microsoft's CEO and executives support ethical AI through the AETHER Committee. This committee evaluates high-impact AI projects for privacy and fairness. Leadership can embed ethics in an organisation, as Microsoft's internal training and industry collaborations set ethical AI standards (Varma *et al.*, 2023). GE Healthcare promotes ethical AI use with patient-centric AI frameworks. GE Healthcare leadership values explainability and accountability in AI diagnostics and patient care. GE's leadership has made it a model for ethical AI use in medicine (Zerfass *et al.*, 2020). AI-driven decisions can severely affect patient outcomes. Organizational ethical AI culture starts with leadership. Leaders can promote responsible AI development and use through ethics, policy, and accountability. Ethical AI adoption improves transparency, accountability, and stakeholder trust, as shown by IBM, Microsoft, and GE Healthcare. Ethical AI leadership will shape a future where AI supports businesses, benefits community interests, and aligns with society.

FUTURE TRENDS IN AI ETHICS

Deep learning, NLP, and predictive analytics raise complex ethical issues. While developing AI Models, developers cannot fully understand the "black box" problem, which leads to serious issues. As models become more complex, transparency and explainability are needed to maintain stakeholder trust (Alam, 2023). AI in sensitive areas like hiring, credit scoring, and criminal justice raises ethical concerns about algorithmic harm. Strong ethics are needed to address biased algorithms, data privacy, and personal data misuse (Cox, 2022). Advanced AI raises questions about human autonomy and decision-making. AI systems are replacing more human tasks, raising concerns about oversight. Artificial intelligence's autonomous decision-making in autonomous driving, healthcare, and customer service has ethical implications, especially when it affects lives. Thus, industry leaders and ethicists emphasize human-centered control and design AI systems to complement human judgment (Hagerty and Rubinov, 2019).

As AI changes industries, business strategies may emphasize ethics. In a responsible innovation market, ethical AI practices differentiate companies. As consumers become more aware of AI's social impact, ethics may become a competitive advantage. AI transparency and accountability can boost consumer trust, loyalty, and brand reputation (Holzinger *et al.*, 2023). Ethics regulations for AI are expected to tighten. The proposed European Artificial Intelligence Act emphasizes accountability, transparency, and human oversight; global regulations are expected. These regulations may require ethical AI framework risk assessments and fairness measures. Anticipate and align regulatory changes to comply and act ethically (Jobin *et al.*, 2019). Ethics for future AI business strategy include inclusive design. AI affects diverse groups, so it must be inclusive. With diverse data sources, inclusive development teams, and stakeholders, AI systems can reduce bias and serve more people. These practices can help companies function ethically, meet social expectations, and innovate inclusively (Kerr *et al.*, 2020).

The Importance of Continuous Adaptation to Societal Expectations

For ethics, businesses must adapt AI practices to changing social norms. AI ethics must change with culture and tech. Companies must assess AI systems for fairness, accountability, and transparency to meet social expectations. Audits, third-party reviews, and dynamic risk assessments can help companies anticipate ethical issues and adjust AI policies (Renda, 2019). AI applications evolve and require constant adaptation. Ethics extend beyond healthcare and finance. Thus, businesses must consider how each AI application affects stakeholders and uphold ethical standards that protect rights and build trust. This can be achieved through ethical AI training, AI development workflow guidelines, and a responsible innovation culture (Yanamala and Suryadevara, 2023). Future AI ethics will address emerging concerns, incorporate ethics into business strategies, and adapt to societal expectations. Businesses that adopt ethical standards and adapt to social changes may benefit financially and operationally as AI drives strategic decision-making. Responsible AI development and use can improve society by aligning its transformative power with fairness, transparency, and accountability.

CONCLUSIONS

This chapter concludes that businesses must ethically integrate AI. AI applications must follow fairness, accountability, transparency, and data privacy to maintain organisational integrity, public trust, and social welfare. Businesses can harm their reputational and operational success by propagating biases, compromising privacy, and eroding stakeholder confidence without proactive commitment to these values. Ethical AI use in business is moral and strategic, helping companies stay competitive and sustainable. The chapter emphasizes leadership and structured oversight for ethical AI practices. Businesses can reduce ethical risks by adopting ethical frameworks, internal protocols, and transparency tools like explainable AI as technology evolves. Practitioners must actively practice inclusive data, accountability audits, and emerging regulations. The chapter promotes AI ethics research to fill industry-specific guidelines and AI's social impact gaps. To create an equitable AI landscape that aligns technological progress with societal values, organizations seeking long-term trust and success must commit to ethical AI as a dynamic process.

REFERENCES

Abulibdeh, A., Zaidan, E., Abulibdeh, R. (2024). Navigating the confluence of artificial intelligence and education for sustainable development in the era of industry 4.0: Challenges, opportunities, and ethical dimensions. *Journal of Cleaner Production.,* Elsevier. *437*, 140527.
[http://dx.doi.org/10.1016/j.jclepro.2023.140527]

Alam, A. (2023). Developing a Curriculum for ethical and responsible AI: A university course on safety, fairness, privacy, and ethics to prepare next generation of ai professionals. *Lecture Notes on Data Engineering and Communications Technologies,* *171*, 879-894.
[http://dx.doi.org/10.1007/978-981-99-1767-9_64]

Aldoseri, A., Al-Khalifa, K.N., Hamouda, A.M. (2023). Re-thinking data strategy and integration for artificial intelligence: concepts, opportunities, and challenges. *Applied Sciences (Switzerland),* *13*(12), 7082.
[http://dx.doi.org/10.3390/app13127082]

Angerschmid, A., Zhou, J., Theuermann, K., Chen, F., Holzinger, A. (2022). Fairness and explanation in AI-informed decision making. *Machine Learning and Knowledge Extraction,* *4*(2), 556-579.
[http://dx.doi.org/10.3390/make4020026]

Ahmad, A.Y.A.B. (2024). Ethical implications of artificial intelligence in accounting: A framework for responsible ai adoption in multinational corporations in Jordan. *International Journal of Data and Network Science,* *8*(1), 401-414.

[http://dx.doi.org/10.5267/j.ijdns.2023.9.014]

Braganza, A., Chen, W., Canhoto, A., Sap, S. (2021). Productive employment and decent work: The impact of AI adoption on psychological contracts, job engagement and employee trust. *Journal of Business Research,* *131*, 485-494.
[http://dx.doi.org/10.1016/j.jbusres.2020.08.018] [PMID: 32836565]

Breidbach, C.F., Maglio, P. (2020). Accountable algorithms? The ethical implications of data-driven business models. *Journal of Service Management,* *31*(2), 163-185.
[http://dx.doi.org/10.1108/JOSM-03-2019-0073]

Campion, A., Gasco-Hernandez, M., Jankin Mikhaylov, S., Esteve, M. (2022). Overcoming the Challenges of Collaboratively Adopting Artificial Intelligence in the Public Sector. *Social Science Computer Review,* *40*(2), 462-477.
[http://dx.doi.org/10.1177/0894439320979953]

Čartolovni, A., Tomičić, A., Lazić Mosler, E. (2022). Ethical, legal, and social considerations of AI-based medical decision-support tools: A scoping review. *International Journal of Medical Informatics,* *161*, 104738.
[http://dx.doi.org/10.1016/j.ijmedinf.2022.104738] [PMID: 35299098]

Chan, A. (2023). GPT-3 and InstructGPT: technological dystopianism, utopianism, and "Contextual" perspectives in AI ethics and industry. *AI and Ethics,* *3*(1), 53-64.
[http://dx.doi.org/10.1007/s43681-022-00148-6]

Cirillo, D., Catuara-Solarz, S., Morey, C., Guney, E., Subirats, L., Mellino, S., Gigante, A., Valencia, A., Rementeria, M.J., Chadha, A.S., Mavridis, N. (2020). Sex and gender differences and biases in artificial intelligence for biomedicine and healthcare. *NPJ Digital Medicine,* *3*, 81.
[http://dx.doi.org/10.1038/s41746-020-0288-5]

Cox, A. (2022). The ethics of AI for information professionals: Eight scenarios. *Journal of the Australian Library and Information Association,* *71*(3), 201-214.
[http://dx.doi.org/10.1080/24750158.2022.2084885]

Curto, G., Jojoa Acosta, M.F., Comim, F., Garcia-Zapirain, B. (2024). Are AI systems biased against the poor? A machine learning analysis using Word2Vec and GloVe embeddings. *JAI and Society,* *39*(2), 617-632.
[http://dx.doi.org/10.1007/s00146-022-01494-z]

Daly, A., Hagendorff, T., Li, H., Mann, M., Marda, V., Wagner, B., Wang, W., & Witteborn, S. (2019). Artificial Intelligence, governance and ethics: Global perspectives. *SSRN Electronic Journal.*
[http://dx.doi.org/10.2139/ssrn.3414805]

Egorenkov, D. (2024). AI-Powered predictive customer lifetime value: maximizing long-term profits. *International Journal of Scientific Research and Management (IJSRM),* *12*(9), 7339-7354.
[http://dx.doi.org/10.18535/ijsrm/v12i09.em02]

Frik, A., Nurgalieva, L., Bernd, J., Lee, J. S., Schaub, F., & Egelman, S. (2019). Privacy and security threat models and mitigation strategies of older adults. *Proceedings of the 15th Symposium on Usable Privacy and Security, SOUPS* 2019, 21–40. Available from: https://www.usenix.org/conference/soups2019/presentation/frik.

Gallardo, A., Choy, C., Juneja, J., Bozkir, E., Cobb, C., Bauer, L., Cranor, L. (2023). Speculative privacy concerns about ar glasses data collection. *Proceedings on Privacy Enhancing Technologies,* *2023*(4), 416-435.
[http://dx.doi.org/10.56553/popets-2023-0117]

Giovanola, B., Tiribelli, S. (2023). Beyond bias and discrimination: redefining the AI ethics principle of fairness in healthcare machine-learning algorithms. *AI and Society,* *38*(2), 549-563.
[http://dx.doi.org/10.1007/s00146-022-01455-6]

Hagerty, A., & Rubinov, I. (2019). Global AI ethics: A review of the social impacts and ethical implications of Artificial Intelligence. *ArXiv Preprint* ArXiv:1907.07892. http://arxiv.org/abs/1907.07892.

Hasija, A., Esper, T.L. (2022). In artificial intelligence (AI) we trust: A qualitative investigation of AI technology acceptance. *Journal of Business Logistics, 43*(3), 388-412.
[http://dx.doi.org/10.1111/jbl.12301]

Holzinger, A., Keiblinger, K., Holub, P., Zatloukal, K., Müller, H. (2023). AI for life: Trends in artificial intelligence for biotechnology. *New Biotechnology.,* Elsevier.*74*, 16-24.
[http://dx.doi.org/10.1016/j.nbt.2023.02.001]

Ingrams, A., Kaufmann, W., Jacobs, D. (2022). In AI we trust? Citizen perceptions of AI in government decision making. *Policy Internet, 14*(2), 390-409.
[http://dx.doi.org/10.1002/poi3.276]

Ioannou, A., Tussyadiah, I., Lu, Y. (2020). Privacy concerns and disclosure of biometric and behavioral data for travel. *International Journal of Information Management, 54*, 102122.
[http://dx.doi.org/10.1016/j.ijinfomgt.2020.102122]

Jobin, A., Ienca, M., Vayena, E. (2019). The global landscape of AI ethics guidelines. *Nature Machine Intelligence, 1*(9), 389-399.
[http://dx.doi.org/10.1038/s42256-019-0088-2]

Kaplan, A., Haenlein, M. (2019). Siri, Siri, in my hand: Who's the fairest in the land? On the interpretations, illustrations, and implications of artificial intelligence. *Business Horizons, 62*(1), 15-25.
[http://dx.doi.org/10.1016/j.bushor.2018.08.004]

Kerr, A., Barry, M., Kelleher, J.D. (2020). Expectations of artificial intelligence and the performativity of ethics: Implications for communication governance. *Big Data and Society, 7*(1).
[http://dx.doi.org/10.1177/2053951720915939]

Kim, B., Park, J., Suh, J. (2020). Transparency and accountability in AI decision support: Explaining and visualizing convolutional neural networks for text information. *Decision Support Systems, 134*, 113302.
[http://dx.doi.org/10.1016/j.dss.2020.113302]

Klimova, B., Pikhart, M., Kacetl, J. (2023). Ethical issues of the use of AI-driven mobile apps for education. *Frontiers in Public Health, 10.*
[http://dx.doi.org/10.3389/fpubh.2022.1118116]

Kunduru, A.R. (2023). Security concerns and solutions for enterprise cloud computing applications. *Asian Journal of Research in Computer Science, 15*(4), 24-33.
[http://dx.doi.org/10.9734/ajrcos/2023/v15i4327]

Lucic, A., Bleeker, M., Jullien, S., Bhargav, S., de Rijke, M. (2022). Reproducibility as a mechanism for teaching fairness, accountability, confidentiality, and transparency in artificial intelligence. *Proceedings of the 36ᵗʰ AAAI Conference on Artificial Intelligence, AAAI 2022, 12792-12800.*
[http://dx.doi.org/10.1609/aaai.v36i11.21558]

Mittelstadt, B. (2019). Principles alone cannot guarantee ethical AI. *Nature Machine Intelligence, 1*(11), 501-507.
[http://dx.doi.org/10.1038/s42256-019-0114-4]

Nassar, A., Kamal, M. (2021). Ethical dilemmas in AI-powered decision-making: a deep dive into big data-driven ethical considerations. *International Journal of Responsible Artificial Intelligence, 11*(8), 1-11. Availble from: https://neuralslate.com/index.php/Journal-of-Responsible-AI/article/view/43

Ntoutsi, E., Fafalios, P., Gadiraju, U., Iosifidis, V., Nejdl, W., Vidal, M.E., Ruggieri, S., Turini, F., Papadopoulos, S., Krasanakis, E., Kompatsiaris, I., Kinder-Kurlanda, K., Wagner, C., Karimi, F., Fernandez, M., Alani, H., Berendt, B., Kruegel, T., Heinze, C., Broelemann, K., Kasneci, G., Tiropanis, T., Staab, S. (2020). Bias in data-driven Artificial Intelligence systems-An introductory survey. *Wiley Interdisciplinary Reviews: Data Mining and Knowledge Discovery, 10*(3), e1356.
[http://dx.doi.org/10.1002/widm.1356]

Peters, D., Vold, K., Robinson, D., Calvo, R.A. (2020). Responsible AI—two frameworks for ethical design

practice. *IEEE Transactions on Technology and Society, 1*(1), 34-47.
[http://dx.doi.org/10.1109/TTS.2020.2974991]

Pratama, A.R., Firmansyah, F.M., Rahma, F. (2022). Security awareness of single sign-on account in the academic community: the roles of demographics, privacy concerns, and Big-Five personality. *Peer J Computer Science, 8*
[http://dx.doi.org/10.7717/peerj-cs.918]

Renda, A. (2019). Artificial intelligence: ethics, governance and policy challenges. In *CEPS Task Force Report*. ceeol.com. Availble from: https://ssrn.com/abstract=3420810.

Rességuier, A., Rodrigues, R. (2020). *AI ethics should not remain toothless!* A call to bring back the teeth of ethics. *Big Data and Society, 7*(2), 2053951720942541.
[http://dx.doi.org/10.1177/2053951720942541]

Roche, C., Wall, P.J., Lewis, D. (2023). Ethics and diversity in artificial intelligence policies, strategies and initiatives. *AI and Ethics, 3*(4), 1095-1115.
[http://dx.doi.org/10.1007/s43681-022-00218-9]

Rohunen, A., Markkula, J. (2019). On the road – listening to data subjects' personal mobility data privacy concerns. *Behaviour and Information Technology, 38*(5), 486-502.
[http://dx.doi.org/10.1080/0144929X.2018.1540658]

Roselli, D., Matthews, J., Talagala, N. (2019). Managing bias in AI. *The Web Conference 2019 - Companion of the World Wide Web Conference, WWW 2019, 539-544.
[http://dx.doi.org/10.1145/3308560.3317590]

Schiff, D., Biddle, J., Borenstein, J., Laas, K. (2020). What's next for AI ethics, policy, and governance? A global overview. *AIES 2020 - Proceedings of the AAAI/ACM Conference on AI, Ethics, and Society, 153-158.
[http://dx.doi.org/10.1145/3375627.3375804]

Serna, I., Morales, A., Fierrez, J., Obradovich, N. (2022). Sensitive loss: Improving accuracy and fairness of face representations with discrimination-aware deep learning. *Artificial Intelligence., Elsevier.305*, 103682.
[http://dx.doi.org/10.1016/j.artint.2022.103682]

Shneiderman, B. (2020). Bridging the gap between ethics and practice: Guidelines for reliable, safe, and trustworthy human-centered AI systems. *ACM Transactions on Interactive Intelligent Systems, 10*(4), 1-31.
[http://dx.doi.org/10.1145/3419764]

Silberman, G. M., Roberts, M. L., Belanger, J., (2020). Detecting and reducing bias (including discrimination) in an automated decision making process. US Patent Availble from: https://patents.google.com/patent/US10861028B2/en%0Ahttps://patentimages.storage.googleapis.com/76/1f/60/12756f804f0ac7/US10861028.pdf.

Taeihagh, A. (2021). Governance of artificial intelligence. *Policy and Society, 40*(2), 137-157.
[http://dx.doi.org/10.1080/14494035.2021.1928377]

Varma, A., Dawkins, C., Chaudhuri, K. (2023). Artificial intelligence and people management: A critical assessment through the ethical lens. *Human Resource Management Review, 33*(1), 100923.
[http://dx.doi.org/10.1016/j.hrmr.2022.100923]

Varona, D., & Suárez, J. L. (2022). Discrimination, Bias, Fairness, and Trustworthy AI. In Applied Sciences (Switzerland) (Vol. 12, Issue 12). mdpi.com.
[http://dx.doi.org/10.3390/app12125826]

Walz, A., & Firth-Butterfield, K. (2019). Implementing ethics into artificial intelligence: a contribution, from legal perspective, to the development of an AI governance regime. Duke Law and Technology Review, 18(1), 176. Availble from: https://heinonline.org/hol-cgi-bin/get_pdf.cgi?handle=hein.journals/dltr18&section=17.

Weber-Lewerenz, B. (2021). Corporate digital responsibility (CDR) in construction engineering—ethical guidelines for the application of digital transformation and artificial intelligence (AI) in user practice. In SN Applied Sciences (Vol. 3, Issue 10..

[http://dx.doi.org/10.1007/s42452-021-04776-1]

Wellner, G., Rothman, T. (2020). Feminist AI: Can We Expect Our AI Systems to Become Feminist? *Philosophy and Technology, 33*(2), 191-205.
[http://dx.doi.org/10.1007/s13347-019-00352-z]

Wilson, C., & van der Velden, M. (2022). Sustainable AI: An integrated model to guide public sector decision-making. In Technology in Society (Vol. 68). Elsevier.
[http://dx.doi.org/10.1016/j.techsoc.2022.101926]

Wirtz, B.W., Weyerer, J.C., Geyer, C. (2019). Artificial Intelligence and the Public Sector—Applications and Challenges. *International Journal of Public Administration, 42*(7), 596-615.
[http://dx.doi.org/10.1080/01900692.2018.1498103]

Yanamala, A. K. Y., & Suryadevara, S. (2023). Advances in Data Protection and Artificial Intelligence: Trends and Challenges. In International Journal of Advanced Engineering Technologies and Innovations (Vol. 1, Issue 01, pp. 294–319). Availble from: https://ijaeti.com/index.php/Journal/article/download/392/407.

Yaseen, A. (2022). Accelerating the Soc: Achieve Greater Efficiency With Ai-Driven Automation. Nternational Journal of Responsible Artificial Intelligence 1 | P a g e Journal of Artificial Intelligence and Machine Learning in Management , 12(1). Availble from: https://orcid.org/0009-0002-8950-0767.

Yaseen, A. (2023). Ai-Driven Threat Detection and Response: a Paradigm Shift in Cybersecurity. *International Journal of Information and Cybersecurity, 7*(12), 25-43. Availble from: https://publications.dlpress.org/index.php/ijic/article/view/73

Zarifis, A., Holland, C. P., & Milne, A. (2023). Evaluating the impact of AI on insurance: the four emerging AI- and data-driven business models. In Emerald Open Research (Vol. 1, Issue 1). emerald.com..
[http://dx.doi.org/10.1108/EOR-01-2023-0001]

Zerfass, A., Hagelstein, J., Tench, R. (2020). Artificial intelligence in communication management: a cross-national study on adoption and knowledge, impact, challenges and risks. *Journal of Communication Management, 24*(4), 377-389.
[http://dx.doi.org/10.1108/JCOM-10-2019-0137]

CHAPTER 4

Data-driven Decision Making: AI's Role in Business Strategy

Abstract: This chapter examines how AI changes data-driven business strategy. As data becomes a strategic asset, AI technologies improve decision-making. The findings indicate that AI significantly improves strategic decision-making, operational efficiency, and customer experiences. By optimizing data analysis, AI enhances business adaptability in complex and rapidly changing environments. The integration of AI not only drives innovation but also fosters sustainable business growth by helping companies remain competitive amid shifting market trends and evolving consumer expectations. AI's role in business strategy will continue to expand as technological advancements unlock new opportunities for growth and transformation.

Keywords: AI, Business strategy, Data-driven, Data privacy, Ethical considerations, Operational efficiency, Sustainable growth.

INTRODUCTION

Data-driven decision-making (DDDM) improves modern business decision-making. Successful companies gain insights from massive data sets. Data guides DDDM's strategic actions to quickly respond to market changes, customer preferences, and operational inefficiencies. Digital firms realise that DDDM improves decision-making in marketing, finance, and operations (Nassar and Kamal, 2021). Data and analytics shape DDDM. Businesses can make informed decisions with user, social media, and operational data. Businesses can identify trends, predict future events, capitalize on opportunities, and mitigate risks using data-driven analysis. Innovation, customer satisfaction, and profitability are better for data-driven companies (Eboigbe *et al.*, 2023).

AI has made data-driven business decisions essential. Artificial intelligence's real-time massive data analysis transformed businesses. Machine learning, deep learning, and natural language processing help AI find patterns, trends, and correlations humans miss. Better predictions and decisions help businesses create more effective strategies (Usman *et al.*, 2024). Analysis of AI data improves business strategies beyond measure. AI-driven insights improve marketing, supply chain, and customer interaction. Amazon and Netflix use AI to predict customer preferences and make personalized recommendations. AI boosts customer engagement and revenue growth, proving its strategic value in decision-making (Rejikumar *et al.*, 2020).

Artificial Intelligence improves personalization and predictive analytics, helping businesses predict consumer behavior. Historical data helps machine learning-based AI models predict future outcomes. Knowing market trends or patient needs helps in finance, healthcare, and retail. Forecasting market changes with AI can help finance firms invest quickly (Javaid, 2024). AI suggests data-driven actions beyond prediction in prescriptive analytics. By analyzing scenarios, AI algorithms suggest the best goal-achieving strategy. This skill helps industries make quick, data-driven decisions. Optimizing delivery routes with AI in real time saves money. Decision-making agility helps companies compete in fast-paced markets (Sarker, 2021).

AI business models allow real-time data analysis. Gathering, cleaning, and analyzing data slowed decision-making. Businesses get real-time insights from AI. Retail and finance need real-time capability. With data-driven decisions, businesses can seize opportunities and avoid mistakes (Machireddy *et al.*, 2021). AI risk management helps businesses. Fraud, cybersecurity, and financial instability can be detected in massive datasets by AI. A proactive risk management helps businesses avoid major issues. Predictions generated by AI improve the accuracy of insurance pricing and mitigate financial risk (Basile *et al.*, 2023).

Data-driven AI decisions improve industry innovation. Product, service, and business model innovations from AI-powered companies can meet changing customer needs. Companies can find market gaps and meet needs by using AI to analyze consumer feedback, market data, and competitor activity. AI-powered innovation helps businesses compete in a fast-changing environment (Johnson *et al.*, 2021). AI business strategy improves operational efficiency. By automating tedious tasks, AI enables employees to focus on strategic thinking and creative work. Assembly line robots with AI can work faster and more accurately than humans, lowering costs and increasing output. Efficiency benefits strategic initiatives like R&D by reducing costs and allocating resources (Ajegbile *et al.*, 2024).

Benefits aside, AI business strategy is difficult. Businesses must responsibly handle customer data under GDPR. Legacy system AI integration is difficult and expensive. Artificial intelligence requires company infrastructure and training. Businesses must fix these issues to maximise AI's data-driven decision-making (Elgendy *et al.*, 2022). Business models using AI raise ethical issues. AI increases data biases, resulting in unfair results. Bad training data has been used to accuse AI-driven hiring tools of discrimination. Trust in AI-driven decision-making requires transparency, fairness, and accountability. Businesses should prioritise ethical AI to avoid legal and reputational issues (Rajagopal *et al*., 2022). Increased data-driven decision-making by AI foreshadows future work impacts. Workers become more strategic, analytical, and creative with AI. AI workers need problem-solving, critical thinking, and data literacy. For better decision-making and long-term success, companies train employees to use AI (Chaudhuri *et al*., 2024).

The purpose of the chapter is to examine the role of artificial intelligence in enhancing business strategies through data-driven decision-making and its impact on organizational performance. The visual depiction of the study's findings is illustrated in Fig. (**1**) below.

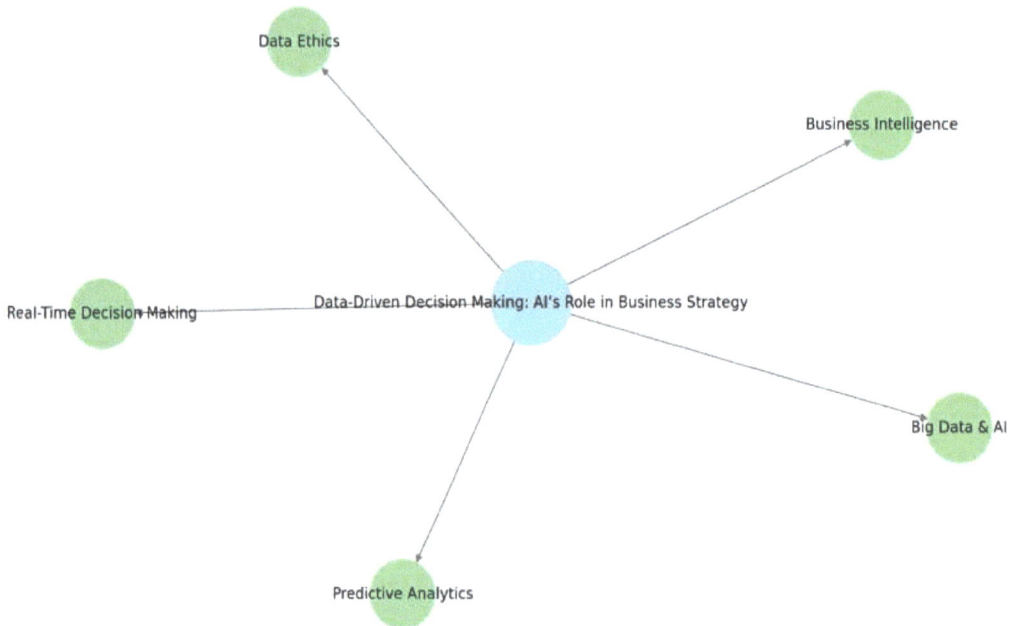

Fig. (1). Conceptual framework.

UNDERSTANDING DATA-DRIVEN DECISION MAKING

Data analysis and interpretation replace intuition, experience, and observation in data-driven decision-making (DDDM). This method informs business decisions through systematic data collection, processing, and analysis. According to DDDM, evidence-based approaches can enhance strategies, improve operational efficiency, and elevate customer experiences. (Bousdekis *et al*., 2021). Data helps companies make better decisions by revealing operations, market trends, and customer behavior. DDDM values data quality, governance, analytical rigor, and experimentation. Data quality emphasises accurate, reliable, and relevant data for trustworthy decision-making (Nassar and Kamal, 2021). Data governance involves data management policies, compliance, and accountability (Kar and Dwivedi, 2020). Analytical rigor involves drawing data conclusions using robust statistical methods. Finally, a culture of experimentation encourages organizations to test hypotheses and iterate on data-driven strategies, fostering innovation and continuous improvement (Wu *et al.*, 2021).

This shift from intuition-based to data-based strategies changes how organizations make decisions. Previously, businesses used to make decisions based on intuition and experience. Though useful, intuition often lacks empirical support for informed decision-making (Sarker, 2021). Better data and analytics enable fact-based decision-making. This change improves strategic decision-making and reduces bias (Saura *et al.*, 2021). Companies realize the importance of a data-driven culture as they adopt DDDM. All employees are encouraged to use data in decision-making and share insights across departments (Phoon *et al.*, 2022). Data analysts and marketing teams may analyze customer behavior and plan campaigns. Collaboration generates new ideas and multiple perspectives, improving decision-making (Reichstein *et al.*, 2019).

DDDM requires data collection, processing, and analysis. Good decision-making requires consistent, relevant data collection (Hosen *et al.*, 2024). Companies must decide what data they need—customer feedback, sales figures, or operational metrics—and set up processes to collect it (Elgendy *et al.*, 2022; Jonas *et al.*, 2024; Mohammed *et al.*, 2024; Yomboi, Majeed, *et al.*, 2024; Yomboi, Mohammed, *et al.*, 2024). Processing organizes and cleans data for analysis. This step is essential for removing inconsistencies and extracting meaningful insights (Troisi *et al.*, 2020). After data collection and processing, DDDM is applied to analyze the information. Descriptive, predictive, and prescriptive analytics help companies spot trends, predict outcomes, and make data-driven recommendations (Olaniyi *et al.*, 2023). Descriptive analytics helps companies understand past performance. Predictive analytics predicts future events using statistical models, while prescriptive analytics recommends actions using data (Matheus *et al.*, 2020).

Decision-making requires data collection, processing, and analysis. Prioritising these elements helps businesses identify trends, satisfy customers, and streamline processes (Akter *et al.*, 2019). Examining buying trends helps stores tailor marketing and inventory to customer preferences, increasing sales and satisfaction. Companies that ignore these practices may miss opportunities and act poorly (Awan *et al.*, 2021). Due to its adaptability and efficiency, DDDM has changed many industries. Patient care and healthcare operations benefit from data-driven approaches. Doctors use data analysis to optimize resource use, identify treatment efficacy trends, and improve patient outcomes (Geng and Xie, 2019). Predictive analytics improves healthcare by predicting patient needs and preventing complications.

Finance is a key area where DDDM is applied. Banks use data analysis to assess credit risk, detect fraud, and personalize customer services (Ooijen *et al.*, 2019). Transaction data and customer behavior allow these firms to customize and lend financial products. Data-driven solutions boost customer satisfaction and lower financial risk, stabilising the sector (Klingenberg *et al.*, 2019). Retail may be the most visible DDDM change. Amazon and Walmart use massive customer data for inventory, pricing, and marketing. Analyzing customer feedback and purchasing behavior can help these retailers improve their products and services. Amazon recommends products based on customer data, increasing sales and loyalty (Bertsimas *et al.*, 2021).

Supply chain management and production optimization benefit from data-driven decision-making. Manufacturers use data analytics to track equipment performance, predict maintenance, and streamline production (Trabucchi and Buganza, 2019). Real-time sensor and machine data analytics improve product quality, efficiency, and downtime. Competitive manufacturing requires proactive decision-making (Ntoutsi *et al.*, 2020). Companies now use data to inform their marketing strategies through data-driven decision-making (DDDM).. Marketing can improve outreach by analyzing customer behavior, engagement metrics, and campaign performance (Mandinach and Schildkamp, 2021). This method boosts conversions and ROI by enabling targeted and personalized marketing. DDDM is changing transportation, especially ride-sharing and autonomous vehicles. Data lets Uber and Lyft optimise routes, manage supply and demand, and improve user experiences (Charnley *et al.*, 2019). Data-driven insights help these companies deploy drivers where they are needed, improving service and customer satisfaction. DDDM transforms HR talent acquisition and management. Data analytics helps companies recruit, evaluate, and retain top talent (Montáns *et al.*, 2019). HR departments can improve employee engagement and productivity by analyzing engagement and performance metrics and making talent development and succession planning decisions. Education was also transformed by DDDM. Student performance, curriculum, and learning are evaluated using data. Using student engagement and achievement data, educators can tailor their teaching strategies to individual learning needs, improving student success (Huber *et al.*, 2019).

DDDM's growing importance across industries emphasizes data-driven strategies for competitiveness. As data grows and analytical technologies advance, DDDM will enable organizations to innovate, improve performance, and leverage insights more effectively (Schildkamp, 2019). In a data-driven world, intuition-based businesses may struggle. Transitioning from intuition to data-driven strategies alters organizational decision-making. Data quality and analytical rigor help organizations make good decisions with DDDM. Good decision-making requires data collection, processing, and analysis. DDDM has transformed many industries, proving that data-driven strategies can compete.

Artificial Intelligence in Business Strategy

AI-driven business strategy is changing how companies operate and compete. AI includes machine, deep, and natural language processing. These technologies can automate processes, give businesses insights from massive data sets, and improve customer interactions. AI improves efficiency, innovation, and customer experience (Nassar and Kamal, 2021). The integration of AI into business strategies is transforming industries and providing a competitive edge to early adopters. Machine learning algorithms let computers learn from data without programming (Sarker, 2021). Fraud detection, customer segmentation, and recommendation systems use this technology. Deep learning analyzes complex data structures with multilayered neural networks, improving image and speech recognition (Hosen *et al.*, 2024). Natural language processing improves business-customer interactions by helping chatbots and virtual assistants understand, interpret, and respond to human language (Elgendy *et al.*, 2022). AI helps companies gain insights and drive data-driven strategic initiatives. Data from various sources overwhelms organizations, making AI essential for data analysis. Traditional data analysis can't handle today's volume, velocity, and variety (Troisi *et al.*, 2020). AI algorithms can quickly explore massive datasets for patterns and trends humans may miss. This helps companies make better decisions, spot opportunities, and adapt to market changes (Awan *et al.*, 2021). AI-based data analysis improves strategic planning and operational efficiency, boosting performance and competitiveness.

How AI Aligns with Business Strategy Development

AI provides decision-making insights to help businesses develop strategies. AI in strategic frameworks helps businesses understand market dynamics, customer behavior, and internal processes. The alignment lets companies use data to find growth opportunities, streamline operations, and optimise resource allocation (Bousdekis *et al.*, 2021). Thus, AI-focused strategic development helps companies adapt to market and consumer changes. Simulating and evaluating scenarios with

AI helps organizations make strategic decisions. AI-based predictive analytics helps businesses predict trends using historical data and market conditions (Kar and Dwivedi, 2020). Companies use predictive models to predict customer needs, optimize inventory, and allocate resources. Prescriptive analytics helps organisations make strategic decisions by recommending actions based on predictive insights (Wu *et al.*, 2021). This lets companies anticipate new trends and challenges, updating their strategies. AI boosts departmental collaboration and data-driven decision-making. Breaking silos and letting cross-functional teams analyse data together helps organisations develop holistic strategies (Saura *et al.*, 2021). To meet customer needs and market demands, marketing, sales, and product development teams can analyze customer data and identify trends. This collaborative approach improves strategic alignment and innovation by creating AI-driven business strategies from diverse perspectives.

Predictive Analytics, Prescriptive Analytics, and AI-powered Decision-making

In AI-powered decision-making, predictive analytics predicts future events using historical data. Businesses can use machine learning algorithms to find trends, correlations, and outcomes in massive data sets (Phoon *et al.*, 2022). Predictive analytics helps retailers optimize inventory, predict customer purchases, and customize marketing campaigns. This proactive approach helps companies make market-driven decisions, improving their competitiveness in the ever-changing business landscape. Prescriptive analytics forecasts and advises on future outcomes. AI and prescriptive analytics help organisations assess multiple scenarios and choose the best option (Reichstein *et al.*, 2019). Rapid decisions help in dynamic situations. Prescriptive analytics helps supply chain managers optimize inventory control and logistics for cost-effective delivery. Prescriptive analytics helps companies make data-driven decisions for efficiency and strategy. Prescriptive analytics helps companies make data-driven decisions to enhance efficiency and guide strategic planning. Both predictive and prescriptive analytics have transformed AI-powered decision-making by automatically analyzing data, reducing human error, and providing real-time operational insights (Karo *et al.*, 2024).This shift enables companies to respond rapidly to consumer preferences, competitive pressures, and changing market conditions. AI-driven decision-making supports success in complex, data-intensive environments.

AI-driven Business Intelligence

AI has made data analysis and smart decisions possible in business intelligence (BI). Machine learning, predictive analytics, and natural language processing aid BI data analysis and interpretation. This enables companies to move beyond manual, data analysis-based business intelligence (BI) and gain more accurate and efficient insights. AI-driven BI quickly provides actionable insights from complex data environments, improving operational efficiency and strategic planning (Machireddy *et al.*, 2021). Business intelligence relies on AI's fast and massive data analysis. Traditional BI systems' slow real-time data processing delays insights and reactive decision-making. Real-time AI analysis helps businesses spot anomalies (Narneg *et al.*, 2024). Businesses can anticipate operational issues, consumer preferences, and market changes. New data helps AI predict and understand (Yablonsky, 2019). Business intelligence systems with AI can boost competitiveness. AI can reveal hidden data patterns about consumer behavior, market dynamics, and operational efficiency (Alnoukari, 2020). Improved plans and decisions can help companies grow and profit. Artificial Intelligence in BI systems boosts marketing, customer service, and operations, giving companies an edge over outdated analysis methods (Eboigbe *et al.*, 2023).

Integration of AI with Business Intelligence Tools

AI and business intelligence improve data-driven decision-making. Many traditional BI applications use error-prone, time-consuming manual data analysis. These tools automate data processing and analysis with AI to give companies faster, more accurate insights (Corea, 2019). Simple AI-powered business intelligence (BI) system interfaces allow business users to interact with complex datasets without requiring technical expertise (Li and Xu, 2022). The integration of AI with BI enables advanced analytics and enhances data accessibility across organizations. AI systems can identify trends, predict outcomes, and make recommendations from past data. This helps businesses move from descriptive to predictive and prescriptive analytics, guiding their actions and future (Usman *et al.*, 2024). Advanced analytics reduce risk, improve decision-making, and seize opportunities (Bharadiya, 2023). Integration of AI biases promotes data-driven business decisions. AI simplifies data interpretation, enabling departmental staff to use it effectively to guide their work. (Machireddy *et al.*, 2021). Data democratisation enables cross-functional collaboration and market agility by empowering all teams to make informed decisions (Paramesha *et al.*, 2024). Companies that adopt data-driven strategies and remain adaptable are more likely to gain a competitive advantage.

How AI Enhances Real-time Data Insights and Trends Identification

AI enhances real-time data insights and identifies business-guiding trends. AI can analyze massive amounts of data in real time using machine learning algorithms, giving organisations insights (Schmitt, 2023). Today's fast-paced business environment requires a quick response to changes, which can affect competitive positioning. Retail and finance companies can real-time track customer behavior and market changes to adjust strategies and operations (Schrettenbrunnner, 2020). Pattern recognition helps AI spot trends. Traditional methods cannot find patterns in historical and real-time data like AI algorithms. AI can detect subtle changes in customer preferences or market demand to help businesses make proactive decisions (Devarasetty, 2023). Trend identification helps companies seize new opportunities, improve customer experiences, and adapt products to market needs (Alghamdi and Al-Baity, 2022). AI enables real-time data visualization, helping decision-makers understand complex data sets (Farayola *et al.*, 2023). AI-enabled BI tools can dynamically visualize KPIs and trends as new data arrives. Companies can make quick, informed decisions using the latest data (Arora *et al.*, 2024). Real-time insights and trend identification from AI can boost strategic agility and competitiveness in fast-changing markets.

Case Studies of Businesses Utilizing AI for Decision-making (Retail, Healthcare, Finance)

Many industries use AI for decision-making, demonstrating its transformative potential. Amazon uses AI to improve inventory, customer personalization, and supply chain operations. Analyzing consumer data and purchase trends will enable Amazon to project demand and change inventory levels, thus lowering surplus stock and lost sales (Chintala and Thiyagarajan, 2023). Using machine learning, their recommendation engine also suggests customized products based on past purchases and browsing behavior that increase sales (Mishra and Tripathi, 2021). Watson Health leverages artificial intelligence to optimize operations and patient care. It assists doctors in diagnosis, prediction, and treatment recommendations by analyzing vast amounts of medical data, including clinical research and electronic health records. By means of comparable cases, Watson can evaluate the medical histories of cancer patients and propose tailored treatment recommendations, thus improving patient outcomes and simplifying healthcare provider decisions (Wamba-Taguimdje *et al.*, 2020). Artificial Intelligence-driven decisions have allowed finance to flourish. Using Artificial Intelligence, financial companies such as JPMorgan Chase spot fraud and control risk. Real-time identification of unusual transaction patterns using artificial Intelligence Algorithms will enable businesses to lower fraud and losses (Emeihe *et al.*, 2024). Credit risk assessments driven by Artificial Intelligence guide lending decisions and help reduce default rates (Chaudhuri *et al.*, 2024). These case studies demonstrate how Artificial Intelligence could enable companies in all spheres to make data-driven decisions meant to increase performance and efficiency.

AI and Competitive Advantage

AI is helping companies compete across industries. AI enhances company productivity, decision-making, and creativity (Wu *et al.*, 2021). AI-driven strategic insights and data analysis help businesses adapt faster to consumer needs and market changes (Nassar and Kamal, 2021). AI can help companies outperform competitors, capitalize on trends, and adapt to fast-changing corporate environments (Awan *et al.*, 2021). AI improves customer satisfaction. AI-driven product personalization boosts customer loyalty and satisfaction (Basile *et al.*, 2023). AI-analyzed consumer preferences and behaviors enable tailored products and marketing. Brand loyalty and customized customer relationships increase sales and market share (Troisi *et al.*, 2020). AI investments will help businesses stand out in saturated markets because consumers want customized interactions. AI maximises resource allocation and cuts costs (Bousdekis *et al.*, 2021). Automating routine tasks and simplifying processes lets companies focus human capital on innovation and growth (Phoon *et al.*, 2022). AI chatbots can answer customer questions, freeing up customer service reps for more complex issues (Rejikumar *et al.*, 2020). Efficiency improves productivity and agility, helping companies adapt to market changes. In conclusion, AI can improve customer satisfaction, operational efficiency, and innovation to give companies an edge.

AI in Strategic Planning

AI lets organizations make decisions using massive amounts of data, changing strategic planning. With AI in strategic planning, companies can gain more insights and predictions. AI algorithms can analyse complex datasets faster than humans, revealing trends and patterns (Bharadiya, 2023). Businesses can use AI-driven analytics to evaluate market conditions, competitive dynamics, and consumer preferences for long-term strategy. Data-driven strategies improve strategic plans and help companies adapt faster to market changes (Wamba-Taguimdje *et al.*, 2020). AI-powered tools let strategic planners simulate and evaluate scenarios. AI-supported scenario analysis let companies test "what-if" scenarios and evaluate strategies (Borges *et al.*, 2021). AI could simulate how economic, regulatory, and competitive factors affect a company's market position. Analysis of multiple scenarios improves resource allocation, product development, and market entry decisions. Predicting challenges and opportunities helps organisations manage uncertainty and build strategic resilience (Campbell *et al.*, 2020). AI enhances strategic planning, but human expertise remains crucial. AI should aid human decision-making and not replace it. Nuanced strategic decisions are difficult for algorithms to capture (Keding, 2021). Strategic planning requires data-driven insights and human intuition. Thus, organizations must encourage human analysts and AI systems to work together and use their strengths to create solid strategic plans that meet goals (Schiff *et al*., 2020).

Use of AI in Forecasting and Scenario Analysis

Companies now predict trends and events using AI. Modern markets are complex and volatile, so linear models and historical data may not predict them (Sharma *et al*., 2024). AI, especially machine learning algorithms, can find complex patterns and relationships in massive datasets to improve forecasting. Social media sentiment, economic indicators, and industry reports improve AI predictions (Allen, 2019). Forecasts improve strategic planning and resource management by enabling proactive decision-making. In scenario analysis, AI improves strategic decision-making. Simulating futures lets companies see how inputs affect strategic goals (Palomares *et al*., 2021). AI generates many options quickly, preparing decision-makers for different outcomes. Consumer spending-based AI can replicate supply chains and retail inventory models. This helps companies adapt to corporate changes (Holmström, 2022). AI-driven scenario analysis and forecasting improve organizations. As data accumulates, feedback loops improve AI model prediction (Gökçeoğlu *et al*., 2023). Businesses can plan and adapt with real-time data. Companies can plan and make better decisions with AI forecasting and scenario analysis (Hemphill, 2021).

AI's Role in Optimizing Resource Allocation and Operational Efficiency

AI boosts organizational resource allocation and efficiency. With predictive analytics and advanced algorithms, businesses can improve resource allocation, operational insights, and inefficiency detection (Stone *et al*., 2020). Companies can forecast demand using AI and past performance data to allocate resources in real time. It increases output, reduces waste, and saves money (Huang and Rust, 2021). AI predicts consumer demand to avoid overstock and stockouts (Fatima *et al*., 2020). AI streamlines and automates repetitive tasks, improving operational efficiency and resource allocation. RPA with AI reduces errors, speeds up tasks, and replaces manual labour (Eriksson *et al*., 2020). Chatbots can handle basic customer service calls, freeing agents to handle more complex issues (Fountaine *et al*., 2019). Automation helps employees focus on higher-value tasks that support organizational goals, improving efficiency and satisfaction. AI-driven analytics reveals operational performance. By monitoring KPIs and real-time data, AI systems identify process improvements, maintenance demand prediction, and bottlenecks (Son *et al*., 2023). By tracking equipment and predicting maintenance needs, AI can optimise manufacturing schedules and reduce downtime (Chiu and Chai, 2020). AI saves long-term growth through cost savings, competitiveness, operational efficiency, and resource allocation.

Strategic Decision-making through AI: Risk Management, Cost Reduction, and Innovation

Strategic risk management, cost control, and creativity benefit from AI. AI-analyzed massive datasets help companies avoid risk and vulnerability (Brock and Wangenheim, 2019). By tracking unusual transaction trends, AI algorithms help financial institutions detect and stop fraud in real time. This boosts consumer trust and protects corporate assets (Hosen *et al.*, 2024). AI-driven strategies save money. AI automates repetitive tasks and optimises resource allocation to save money and increase efficiency (Yablonsky, 2019). Predicting demand and supplier performance with AI maximizes supply chain inventory and holding costs. This data-driven approach saves businesses money without compromising service (Rajagopal *et al.*, 2022). Efficiency will enable AI-driven cost-cutting plans to help businesses compete. Testing new business models, products, and services with AI helps companies innovate. Artificial intelligence can identify market gaps and inspire new ideas using consumer preferences and market trends (Schrettenbrunnner, 2020). Using consumer feedback and sentiment analysis, AI can develop and market new products that meet consumer expectations (Corea, 2019). Innovative AI-driven industries.

The Importance of Human-AI Collaboration in Strategic Planning

AI is useful, but strategic planning requires human-AI collaboration. While AI can make decisions and analyze data, strategic interpretation and application require human expertise (Machireddy *et al.*, 2021). Human strategists and AI can make better decisions because intuition and creativity balance AI's analysis. Human analysts can provide context and ethics that AI may miss, ensuring strategic decisions match corporate values and goals (Ajegbile *et al.*, 2024). AI-human collaboration improves lifelong learning and knowledge sharing. Data-driven teaching with AI improves creativity and analysis (Mishra and Tripathi, 2021). Collaboration improves decision-making and creates an adaptable workforce (Farayola *et al.*, 2024). Companies in trouble can benefit from human judgment and AI analytics. Cooperation between humans and AI requires clear communication, a supportive culture, and training. Workers need AI tools to maximise strategic planning benefits (Saura *et al.*, 2021). To dynamically combine human knowledge with AI-driven insights, organizations should encourage staff to share ideas and challenge AI recommendations. AI strategic planning, innovation and competitiveness increase with human collaborations (Chaudhuri *et al.*, 2024).

CHALLENGES OF IMPLEMENTING AI IN BUSINESS STRATEGY

Using AI in strategy presents many challenges for corporations. AI and infrastructure investment are major issues. AI development and application take time, money, and skills. Businesses struggle with AI implementation costs like buying expensive hardware and software, hiring qualified professionals, and training them (Vaio *et al.*, 2020). AI will change resource distribution, so companies must adapt their plans and skills (Haleem *et al.*, 2022). Corporate goals must guide AI implementation. Companies use AI explanations. Business-failing AI applications waste resources and miss opportunities (Maedche *et al.*, 2019). Companies should involve key players to align AI deployment strategies with corporate priorities and reduce risk. Cooperation inspires workers and helps companies find the best AI applications (Borges *et al.*, 2021). Last, creating an AI-friendly corporate culture is hard. AI ignorance or job displacement may make workers oppose AI (Cheatham *et al.*, 2019). Change management promotes AI's potential to solve these issues. Training AI system employees reduces adoption uncertainty and resistance (Wirtz *et al.*, 2019). Companies can use AI optimistically.

Data Privacy and Security Concerns

Business strategy requires AI security and privacy. Companies must address data protection and privacy as they train AI systems with more data (Marr and Ward, 2019). AI projects must prioritize data privacy to avoid GDPR fines and legal issues (Wu *et al.*, 2022). To avoid usage and breaches, companies must use strong data governance systems to gather, store, and handle data. AI accesses sensitive data like customer data, increasing data breach risk (Sjödin *et al.*, 2021). A breach can affect a brand's finances and reputation for years (Brunetti *et al.*, 2020). Security audits, access limits, and encryption reduce risks. Companies must monitor new cybersecurity threats and update security systems to avoid vulnerabilities (Sharma *et al.*, 2024). Artificial intelligence data use affects company ethics. Data collection must respect privacy rights and train AI algorithms on diverse datasets to avoid bias and discrimination (Benbya *et al.*, 2020). Legal compliance and public trust require ethical data use and AI development. AI can address data privacy and security concerns for companies and consumers (Enholm *et al.*, 2022).

Integration Issues with Legacy Systems

AI-using businesses struggle to integrate AI with legacy systems. Many businesses use outdated IT infrastructure that cannot support modern AI technologies, making integration difficult and resource-intensive (Holmström, 2022). Data silos from legacy systems' incompatibility with advanced AI tools make data sharing and analysis difficult (Jöhnk *et al.*, 2021). This issue can delay AI implementation and reduce the company's AI benefits. AI integration into workflows and processes may require major operational changes. Retraining employees may be needed to integrate AI systems into workflows (Lee *et al.*, 2019). Employees who prefer traditional methods or worry about AI may be annoyed. Gradual integration and employee discussions and training should promote AI-legacy system acceptance and collaboration (Shaw *et al.*, 2019). Modernising IT infrastructure aids integration. Cloud-based solutions that scale and adapt AI applications and improve data management may be needed (Brock and Wangenheim, 2019). AI integration is gradual and reduces business disruptions. To maximize AI investment value, organizations must proactively address integration challenges to align AI initiatives with existing systems and processes.

Ethical Considerations and Biases in AI Algorithms

Companies using AI in business strategy must address ethics and algorithm biases. Biased AI data can yield biased results (Bharadiya, 2023). Biased algorithms can perpetuate social inequality in hiring, lending, and law enforcement, according to (Nam *et al.*, 2021). Companies must audit algorithms and implement fairness metrics to reduce AI bias (Chan and Zary, 2019). Ethics include transparency and accountability beyond bias. Companies struggle to explain and defend AI decisions as AI systems become more autonomous (Cao, 2023). Untrustworthy AI system decisions must be overcome by transparency with clients and employees. To understand and hold AI-driven decisions accountable, businesses should explain AI algorithms to stakeholders (Strohm *et al.*, 2020). AI ethics, especially consent and privacy, concern companies. AI uses personal data, raising privacy and surveillance concerns (Hangl *et al.*, 2023). To address these ethical issues, companies should create AI ethical frameworks that reflect society's values. Businesses can improve their business strategies and promote justice and openness by building responsible artificial intelligence systems that address ethical issues and prejudices.

Organizational Resistance to AI Adoption

To adopt AI, companies must overcome organizational resistance. Due to job displacement concerns, AI ignorance, or mistrust of its benefits, workers may oppose AI projects (Hemphill, 2021). Aversion to AI tools or deployment can slow development and reduce AI's benefits (Regona *et al.*, 2022). Companies must promote AI as improving human skills rather than replacing them to overcome this resistance. Companies should prioritize communication and education to explain AI technologies and applications to overcome organizational

AI adoption resistance. AI training reduces job loss concerns and improves performance (Sharma *et al.*, 2022). AI implementation with employee participation reduces resistance, increases ownership and commitment, and fosters cooperation (Stone *et al.*, 2020). Leadership commitment drives organizational AI adoption. Leaders who promote AI benefits and commit to integrating AI into business strategies are more likely to get employees on board (Tarafdar *et al.*, 2020). Leaders should emphasize that AI improves human decision-making and creativity and support employees during the transition. By fostering acceptance and proving its value, organizations can adopt AI.

FUTURE TRENDS AND OPPORTUNITIES

Business strategy is changing due to AI, data analytics, and automation. AI will analyse massive data sets for better decision-making and personalisation. According to Wu *et al.*, 2022, better machine learning algorithms can predict customer needs and market trends. IoT and AI will improve operations and supply chain management by collecting and analyzing real-time data. These technologies help companies adapt faster to market changes and consumer demands, giving them an edge. Sustainability is another trendy business strategy. Sustainable operations are becoming more important as consumers go green. Companies are studying renewable energy and circular economy solutions to reduce carbon emissions (Luan *et al.*, 2020). This shift distinguishes brands, attracts socially conscious customers, and boosts reputation. Sustainability regulations and stakeholder expectations will promote sustainable business practices, emphasizing environmental considerations in strategic decision-making. Agile and resilient business strategies are coming. Post-COVID-19 organisations must adapt to new challenges (Bharadiya, 2023). Innovation and flexibility help companies handle disruptions and seize opportunities. Remote work and digital collaboration tools contribute to building organizational resilience (Regona *et al.*, 2022). Embracing technology, sustainability, and agility enables businesses to thrive in dynamic environments.

CONCLUSION

Data-driven decision-making is transformed by AI's fast and accurate analysis of massive data sets. Machine learning and advanced algorithms improve strategic decisions, operational efficiency, and customer experiences. Switching from intuition to evidence-based strategies helps companies meet market and consumer demands. By improving decision-making and innovation, AI helps companies compete in complex and changing environments. Sustainable business growth requires AI involvement. AI helps companies thrive as markets and consumer expectations change. AI will grow in business strategy as technology advances.

AI will boost operational efficiency and open new growth and innovation avenues, ensuring future relevance and resilience. Business success and sustainability in this fast-changing environment depend on AI adoption.

REFERENCES

Akter, S., Bandara, R., Hani, U., Fosso Wamba, S., Foropon, C., Papadopoulos, T. (2019). Analytics-based decision-making for service systems: A qualitative study and agenda for future research. *International Journal of Information Management, 48*, 85-95.
[http://dx.doi.org/10.1016/j.ijinfomgt.2019.01.020]

Alghamdi, N.A., Al-Baity, H.H. (2022). Augmented analytics driven by AI: A digital transformation beyond business intelligence. *Sensors (Basel, Switzerland), 22*(20), 8071.
[http://dx.doi.org/10.3390/s22208071]

Allen, G. C. (2019). Understanding China's AI strategy: Clues to chinese strategic thinking on artificial intelligence and national security. In *Center for a New American Security* (Issue February, pp. 1–22). globalhha.com. Available from: https://www.cnas.org/publications/reports/understanding-chinas-ai-strategy.

Alnoukari, M. (2020). From Business Intelligence to big data: The power of analytics. In: Azevedo, A, Santos, MF (eds). JIntegration Challenges for Analytics, Business Intelligence, and Data Mining (pp. 44–62).
[http://dx.doi.org/10.4018/978-1-7998-5781-5.ch003]

Arora, S., Thota, S. R., & Gupta, S. (2024). Artificial Intelligence-driven big data analytics for business Intelligence in SaaS products. *2024 First International Conference on Pioneering Developments in Computer Science & Digital Technologies (IC2SDT),*Delhi, India, 2024, pp. 164-169. Available from: https://ieeexplore.ieee.org/abstract/ document/10696409/.

Awan, U., Shamim, S., Khan, Z., Zia, N.U., Shariq, S.M., Khan, M.N. (2021). Big data analytics capability and decision-making: The role of data-driven insight on circular economy performance. *Technological Forecasting and Social Change, 168*, 120766.
[http://dx.doi.org/10.1016/j.techfore.2021.120766]

Ajegbile M.D., Olaboye J.A., Maha C.C., Igwama G.T., Abdul, S. (2024). Integrating business analytics in healthcare: Enhancing patient outcomes through data-driven decision making. *World Journal of Biology Pharmacy and Health Sciences 19,* 1, pp. 243–250.
[http://dx.doi.org/10.30574/wjbphs.2024.19.1.0436]

Basile, L.J., Carbonara, N., Pellegrino, R., Panniello, U. (2023). Business intelligence in the healthcare industry: The utilization of a data-driven approach to support clinical decision making. *Technovation, 120*, 102482.
[http://dx.doi.org/10.1016/j.technovation.2022.102482]

Benbya, H., Davenport, T.H., Pachidi, S. (2020). Special issue editorial: Artificial Intelligence in organizations: Current state and future opportunities. *MIS Quarterly Executive, 19*(4), ix-xxi. Available from: https://papers.ssrn.com/sol3/papers.cfm?abstract_id=3741983

Bertsimas, D., Boussioux, L., Cory-Wright, R., Delarue, A., Digalakis, V., Jacquillat, A., Kitane, D. L., Lukin, G., Li, M., Mingardi, L., Nohadani, O., Orfanoudaki, A., Papalexopoulos, T., Paskov, I., Pauphilet, J., Lami, O. S., Stellato, B., Bouardi, H. T., Carballo, K. V., … Zeng, C. (2021). From predictions to prescriptions: A data-driven response to COVID-19. *Health Care Management Science24,* 2, pp. 253–272).
[http://dx.doi.org/10.1007/s10729-020-09542-0]

Bharadiya, J. P. (2023). Machine learning and AI in business intelligence: Trends and opportunities. In *International Journal of Computer (IJC).* researchgate.net. Available from: https://www.researchgate. net/profile/Jasmin-Bharadiya-4/publication/371902170_Machine_Learning_and_AI_in_Business_ Intelligence_Trends_and_Opportunities/links/649afb478de7ed28ba5c99bb/Machine-Learning-a-d-AI-in-Business-Intelligence-Tren-s-and-Opportunities.pdf?origin=journalDetail&_tp=eyJwYWdlIjoiam91cm5hbERldGFpbCJ9.

Borges, A.F.S., Laurindo, F.J.B., Spínola, M.M., Gonçalves, R.F., Mattos, C.A. (2021). The strategic use of artificial intelligence in the digital era: Systematic literature review and future research directions. *International Journal of Information Management, 57*, 102225.
[http://dx.doi.org/10.1016/j.ijinfomgt.2020.102225]

Bousdekis, A., Lepenioti, K., Apostolou, D., & Mentzas, G. (2021). A review of data-driven decision-making methods for industry 4.0 maintenance applications. *Electronics10* (7), 828.
[http://dx.doi.org/10.3390/electronics10070828]

Br. Karo, M., Miller, B.P., Al-Kamari, O.A. (2024). Leveraging data utilization and predictive analytics: Driving innovation and enhancing decision making through ethical governance. *International Transactions on Education Technology, 2*(2), 152-162.
[http://dx.doi.org/10.33050/itee.v2i2.593]

Brock, J.K.U., von Wangenheim, F. (2019). Demystifying AI: What digital transformation leaders can teach you about realistic artificial intelligence. *California Management Review, 61*(4), 110-134.
[http://dx.doi.org/10.1177/1536504219865226]

Brunetti, F., Matt, D. T., Bonfanti, A., De Longhi, A., Pedrini, G., & Orzes, G. (2020). Digital transformation challenges: strategies emerging from a multi-stakeholder approach. *TQM Journal 32*, 4, pp. 697–724.
[http://dx.doi.org/10.1108/TQM-12-2019-0309]

Campbell, C., Sands, S., Ferraro, C., Tsao, H.Y.J., Mavrommatis, A. (2020). From data to action: How marketers can leverage AI. *Business Horizons, 63*(2), 227-243.
[http://dx.doi.org/10.1016/j.bushor.2019.12.002]

Cao, L. (2023). AI in finance: Challenges, techniques, and opportunities. *ACM Computing Surveys, 55*(3), 1-38.
[http://dx.doi.org/10.1145/3502289]

Chan, K. S., & Zary, N. (2019). Applications and Challenges of Implementing Artificial Intelligence in Medical Education: Integrative Review. *JMIR Medical Education 5*, 1, p. e13930. Available from: mededu.jmir.org.
[http://dx.doi.org/10.2196/13930]

Charnley, F., Tiwari, D., Hutabarat, W., Moreno, M., Okorie, O., & Tiwari, A. (2019). Simulation to enable a data-driven circular economy. *Sustainability, 11*(12), 3379.
[http://dx.doi.org/10.3390/su11123379]

Chaudhuri, R., Chatterjee, S., Vrontis, D., Thrassou, A. (2024). Adoption of robust business analytics for product innovation and organizational performance: the mediating role of organizational data-driven culture. *Annals of Operations Research, 339*(3), 1757-1791.
[http://dx.doi.org/10.1007/s10479-021-04407-3]

Cheatham, B., Javanmardian, K., & Samandari, H. (2019). Confronting the risks of artificial intelligence. *McKinsey Quarterly 2019*, 2. Available from: https://www.sipotra.it/wp-content/uploads/2019/05/Confronting-the-risks-of-artificial-intelligence.pdf.

Chintala, S., & Thiyagarajan, V. (2023). AI-Driven Business Intelligence: Unlocking the Future of Decision-Making. *ESP International Journal of Advancements in Computational Technology, 1*, 2, pp 73-84. Available from: https://www.espjournals.org/IJACT/2023/Volume1-Issue2/IJACT-V1I2P108.pdf.

Chiu, T. K. F., & Chai, C. S. (2020). Sustainable curriculum planning for artificial intelligence education: A self-determination theory perspective. *Sustainability, 12*(14), 5568.
[http://dx.doi.org/10.3390/su12145568]

Corea, F. (2019). *Applied Artificial Intelligence: Where AI can be used in business* (Issue Nakamoto 2008). Springer.
[http://dx.doi.org/10.1007/978-3-319-77252-3]

Devarasetty, N. (2023). AI and Data Engineering: Harnessing the Power of Machine Learning in Data-Driven Enterprises. *International Journal of Machine Learning Research in Cybersecurity and Artificial Intelligence.*

14, 1. Available from: http://ijmlrcai.com/index.php/Journal/article/view/68.

Eboigbe, E.O., Farayola, O.A., Olatoye, F.O., Nnabugwu, O.C., Daraojimba, C. (2023). Business intelligence transformation through AI and data analytics. *Engineering Science & Technology Journal, 4*(5), 285-307. [http://dx.doi.org/10.51594/estj.v4i5.616]

Emeihe, E.V., Nwankwo, E.I., Ajegbile, M.D., Olaboye, J.A., Maha, C.C. (2024). The impact of artificial intelligence on regulatory compliance in the oil and gas industry. *International Journal of Life Science Research Archive, 7*(1), 28-39.

Elgendy, N., Elragal, A., Päivärinta, T. (2022). DECAS: a modern data-driven decision theory for big data and analytics. *Journal of Decision Systems, 31*(4), 337-373. [http://dx.doi.org/10.1080/12460125.2021.1894674]

Enholm, I. M., Papagiannidis, E., Mikalef, P., & Krogstie, J. (2022). Artificial Intelligence and business value: A literature review. *Information Systems Frontiers 24,* 5, pp. 1709–1734. [http://dx.doi.org/10.1007/s10796-021-10186-w]

Eriksson, T., Bigi, A., & Bonera, M. (2020). Think with me, or think for me? On the future role of artificial intelligence in marketing strategy formulation. *TQM Journa 32,* 4, pp. 795–814. [http://dx.doi.org/10.1108/TQM-12-2019-0303]

Farayola, O.A., Adaga, E.M., Egieya, Z.E., Ewuga, S.K., Abdul, A.A., Abrahams, T.O. (2024). Advancements in predictive analytics: A philosophical and practical overview. *World Journal of Advanced Research and Reviews, 21*(3), 240-252. [http://dx.doi.org/10.30574/wjarr.2024.21.3.2706]

Fatima, S., Desouza, K.C., Dawson, G.S. (2020). National strategic artificial intelligence plans: A multi-dimensional analysis. *Economic Analysis and Policy, 67*, 178-194. [http://dx.doi.org/10.1016/j.eap.2020.07.008]

Fountaine, T., McCarthy, B., & Saleh, T. (2019). Building the AI-powered organization. In *Harvard Business Review.* wuyuansheng.com. Available from: https://wuyuansheng.com/doc/Databricks-AI-Power-d-Org__Article-Licensing-July21-1.pdf.

Farayola, O.A., Abdul, A.A., Irabor, B.O., Okeleke, E.C. (2023). Innovative business models driven by AI technologies: A review. *Computer Science & IT Research Journal, 4*(2), 85-110. [http://dx.doi.org/10.51594/csitrj.v4i2.608]

Geng, X., Xie, L. (2019). Data-driven decision making in power systems with probabilistic guarantees: Theory and applications of chance-constrained optimization. *Annual Reviews in Control, 47*, 341-363. [http://dx.doi.org/10.1016/j.arcontrol.2019.05.005]

Gökçeoğlu, Y. S., İncesu, A. N., Anarat, F. B., & Akgül, T. (2023). Incorporating Information Architecture (ia), Enterprise Engineering (ee) and Artificial Intelligence (ai) to Improve Business Plans for Small Businesses in the United States. *Journal of Knowledge Learning and Science Technology* ISSN: 2959-6386 (Online), 2(1), 115–127. Available from: https://jklst.org/index.php/home/article/view/113.

Haleem, A., Javaid, M., Qadri, M. A., Singh, R. P., & ... (2022). Artificial intelligence (AI) applications for marketing: A literature-based study. *International Journal of Intelligent Networks 3,* pp 119-132. Available from: https://www.sciencedirect.com/science/article/pii/S2666603022000136. [http://dx.doi.org/10.1016/j.ijin.2022.08.005]

Hangl, J., Krause, S., Behrens, V.J. (2023). Drivers, barriers and social considerations for AI adoption in SCM. *Technology in Society, 74*, 102299. [http://dx.doi.org/10.1016/j.techsoc.2023.102299]

Hemphill, T. A. (2021). Book review: Competing in the age of AI: Strategy and leadership when Algorithms and networks run the world. *Journal of General Management 46,* 4, pp. 322–323. Harvard Business Press. [http://dx.doi.org/10.1177/0306307020972520]

Holmström, J. (2022). From AI to digital transformation: The AI readiness framework. *Business Horizons 65,* 3, pp. 329–339.

[http://dx.doi.org/10.1016/j.bushor.2021.03.006]

Hosen, M.S., Islam, R., Naeem, Z., Folorunso, E.O., Chu, T.S., Al Mamun, M.A., Orunbon, N.O. (2024). Data-driven decision making: Advanced database systems for business intelligence. *Nanotechnology Perceptions, 20*(S3), 687-704.
[http://dx.doi.org/10.62441/nano-ntp.v20iS3.51]

Huang, M. H., & Rust, R. T. (2021). A strategic framework for artificial intelligence in marketing. *Journal of the Academy of Marketing Science 49,* 1, pp. 30–50 .
[http://dx.doi.org/10.1007/s11747-020-00749-9]

Huber, J., Müller, S., Fleischmann, M., & Stuckenschmidt, H (2019). A data-driven newsvendor problem: From data to decision. *European Journal of Operational Research 278,* 3, pp 904-915. Available from: https://www.sciencedirect.com/science/article/pii/S0377221719303807.

Javaid, H. A. (2024). AI-driven predictive analytics in finance: Transforming risk assessment and decision-making. Advances in Computer Sciences, 7. Available from: https://academicpinnacle.com/index.php/acs/article/view/204.

Jöhnk, J., Weißert, M., & Wyrtki, K. (2021). Ready or Not, AI Comes— An Interview Study of Organizational AI Readiness Factors. *European Journal of Operational Research 278,* 3, pp 904-915.
[http://dx.doi.org/10.1007/s12599-020-00676-7]

Johnson, M., Jain, R., Brennan-Tonetta, P., Swartz, E., Silver, D., Paolini, J., Mamonov, S., Hill, C. (2021). Impact of big data and artificial intelligence on industry: Developing a workforce roadmap for a data driven economy. *Global Journal of Flexible Systems Management, 22*(3), 197-217.
[http://dx.doi.org/10.1007/s40171-021-00272-y]

Jonas, Y., Kwasi, N., Elijah Kutogichiga, A., & Kupule Adobauru, F. G. (2024). Digital Transformation of African SMEs: Understanding Digital Transformation. *Digital Transformation in African SMEs: Emerging Issues and Trends,* 61–72.
[http://dx.doi.org/10.2174/9789815223347124020006]

Kar, A.K., Dwivedi, Y.K. (2020). Theory building with big data-driven research – Moving away from the "What" towards the "Why". *International Journal of Information Management, 54,* 102205.
[http://dx.doi.org/10.1016/j.ijinfomgt.2020.102205]

Keding, C. (2021). Understanding the interplay of artificial intelligence and strategic management: four decades of research in review. *Management Review Quarterly, 71*(1), 91-134.
[http://dx.doi.org/10.1007/s11301-020-00181-x]

Klingenberg, C.O., Borges, M.A.V., Antunes, J.A.V., Jr (2019). Industry 4.0 as a data-driven paradigm: a systematic literature review on technologies. *Journal of Manufacturing Technology Management, 32*(3), 570-592.
[http://dx.doi.org/10.1108/JMTM-09-2018-0325]

Lee, J., Suh, T., Roy, D., & Baucus, M. (2019). Emerging technology and business model innovation: The case of artificial intelligence. *Journal of Open Innovation: Technology, Market, and Complexity 5,* 3.
[http://dx.doi.org/10.3390/joitmc5030044]

Li, F., Xu, G. (2022). AI-driven customer relationship management for sustainable enterprise performance. *Sustainable Energy Technologies and Assessments, 52,* 102103.
[http://dx.doi.org/10.1016/j.seta.2022.102103]

Luan, H., Geczy, P., Lai, H., Gobert, J., Yang, S. J. H., Ogata, H., Baltes, J., Guerra, R., Li, P., & Tsai, C. C. (2020). Challenges and future directions of big data and Artificial Intelligence in education. *Frontiers in Psychology Vol. 11.*
[http://dx.doi.org/10.3389/fpsyg.2020.580820]

Machireddy, J. R., Rachakatla, S. K., & (2021a). AI-Driven business analytics for financial forecasting: Integrating data warehousing with predictive models. *Journal of Machine Learning in Pharmaceutical Research 1,* 2. Available from: https://pharmapub.org/index.php/jmlpr/article/view/19.

Machireddy, J. R., Rachakatla, S. K., & Ravichandran, P (2021b). Leveraging AI and machine learning for data-driven business strategy: a comprehensive framework for analytics integration. *African Journal of Artificial Intelligence and Sustainable Development 1,* 2. Available from: https://africansciencegroup.com/index.php/AJAISD/article/view/126.

Maedche, A., Legner, C., Benlian, A., Berger, B., Gimpel, H., Hess, T., Hinz, O., Morana, S., Söllner, M. (2019). AI-based digital assistants. *Business and Information Systems Engineering, 61*(4), 535-544. [http://dx.doi.org/10.1007/s12599-019-00600-8]

Mohammed, M., Yomboi, J., Fataw, A., & Seidu, A. (2024). Future of customer engagement through marketing intelligence. *Utilizing Technology for Sustainable Resource Management Solutions, 308–321.* [http://dx.doi.org/10.4018/979-8-3693-2346-5.ch020]

Mandinach, E.B., Schildkamp, K. (2021). Misconceptions about data-based decision making in education: An exploration of the literature. *Studies in Educational Evaluation., 69,* 100842. [http://dx.doi.org/10.1016/j.stueduc.2020.100842]

Marr, B., & Ward, M. (2019). *Artificial intelligence in practice : how 50 successful companies used artificial intelligence to solve problems.* books.google.com. Available from: books.google.com https://books.google.com/books?hl=en&lr=&id=UbaIDwAAQBAJ&oi=fnd&pg=PA1&dq=Marr,+2016++AI &ots=rOQKQG_QH2&sig=3gYJLts8eG0qK5KCs53bUFCXea4%0Ahttps://books.google.com/books/about/ Artificial_Intelligence_in_Practice.html?id=A62SDwAAQBAJ.

Matheus, R., Janssen, M., & Maheshwari, D. (2020). Data science empowering the public: Data-driven dashboards for transparent and accountable decision-making in smart cities. In Government Information Quarterly (Vol. 37, Issue 3). Elsevier. [http://dx.doi.org/10.1016/j.giq.2018.01.006]

Mishra, S., & Tripathi, A. R. (2021). AI business model: An integrative business approach. *Journal of Innovation and Entrepreneurship 10,* 18. [http://dx.doi.org/10.1186/s13731-021-00157-5]

Montáns, F. J., Chinesta, F., Gómez-Bombarelli, R., & Kutz, J. N. (2019). Data-driven modeling and learning in science and engineering. *Comptes Rendus - Mecanique 347,* 11, pp. 845–855. [http://dx.doi.org/10.1016/j.crme.2019.11.009]

Nam, K., Dutt, C.S., Chathoth, P., Daghfous, A., Khan, M.S. (2021). The adoption of artificial intelligence and robotics in the hotel industry: prospects and challenges. *Electronic Markets, 31*(3), 553-574. [http://dx.doi.org/10.1007/s12525-020-00442-3]

Narneg, S., Adedoja, T., & ... (2024). AI-driven decision support systems in management: Enhancing strategic planning and execution. *International Journal on Recent and Innovation Trends in Computing and Communication.* Available from: https://www.researchgate.net/profile/Suresh-Dodda/publication /383950090_AI-Driven_Decision_Support_Systems_in_Management_Enhancing_Strategic_Planning_ and_Execution/links/66e25265bd20173667cacb87/AI-Driven-Decision-Support-Systems-in-Management - Enhancing-Strategic-Planning-and-Execution.pdf.

Nassar, A., Kamal, M. (2021). Ethical dilemmas in AI-powered decision-making: A deep dive into big data-driven ethical considerations. *International Journal of Responsible Artificial Intelligence, 11*(8), 1-11.Available from: https://neuralslate.com/index.php/Journal-of-Responsible-AI/article/view/43. (2021).

Ntoutsi, E., Fafalios, P., Gadiraju, U., Iosifidis, V., Nejdl, W., Vidal, M.E., Ruggieri, S., Turini, F., Papadopoulos, S., Krasanakis, E., Kompatsiaris, I., Kinder-Kurlanda, K., Wagner, C., Karimi, F., Fernandez, M., Alani, H., Berendt, B., Kruegel, T., Heinze, C., Broelemann, K., Kasneci, G., Tiropanis, T., Staab, S. (2020). Bias in data-driven artificial intelligence systems—An introductory survey. *Wiley Interdisciplinary Reviews: Data Mining and Knowledge Discovery, 10*(3), e1356. [http://dx.doi.org/10.1002/widm.1356]

Olaniyi, O.O., Okunleye, O.J., Olabanji, S.O. (2023). Advancing data-driven decision-making in smart cities through big data analytics: A comprehensive review of existing literature. *Current Journal of Applied Science*

and Technology, 42(25), 10-18.
[http://dx.doi.org/10.9734/cjast/2023/v42i254181]

Palomares, I., Martínez-Cámara, E., Montes, R., García-Moral, P., Chiachio, M., Chiachio, J., Alonso, S., Melero, F. J., Molina, D., Fernández, B., Moral, C., Marchena, R., de Vargas, J. P., & Herrera, F. (2021). A panoramic view and swot analysis of artificial intelligence for achieving the sustainable development goals by 2030: progress and prospects. *Applied Intelligence 51,* 9, pp. 6497–6527.
[http://dx.doi.org/10.1007/s10489-021-02264-y]

Paramesha, M., Rane, N., & Rane, J. (2024). Big data analytics, artificial intelligence, machine learning, internet of things, and blockchain for enhanced business intelligence. *SSRN Electronic Journal.*
[http://dx.doi.org/10.2139/ssrn.4855856]

Phoon, K.K., Ching, J., Shuku, T. (2022). Challenges in data-driven site characterization. *Georisk: Assessment and Management of Risk for Engineered Systems and Geohazards, 16*(1), 114-126.
[http://dx.doi.org/10.1080/17499518.2021.1896005]

Rajagopal, N.K., Qureshi, N.I., Durga, S., Ramirez Asis, E.H., Huerta Soto, R.M., Gupta, S.K., Deepak, S. (2022). Future of business culture: An Artificial Intelligence-driven digital framework for organization decision-making process. *Complexity, 2022*(1), 7796507.
[http://dx.doi.org/10.1155/2022/7796507]

Regona, M., Yigitcanlar, T., Xia, B., & Li, R. Y. M. (2022). Opportunities and Adoption Challenges of AI in the Construction Industry: A PRISMA Review. *Journal of Open Innovation: Technology, Market, and Complexity 8,* 1, 45.
[http://dx.doi.org/10.3390/joitmc8010045]

Reichstein, M., Camps-Valls, G., Stevens, B., Jung, M., Denzler, J., Carvalhais, N., Prabhat, (2019). Deep learning and process understanding for data-driven Earth system science. *Nature, 566*(7743), 195-204.
[http://dx.doi.org/10.1038/s41586-019-0912-1] [PMID: 30760912]

Rejikumar, G., Aswathy Asokan, A., Sreedharan, V.R. (2020). Impact of data-driven decision-making in Lean Six Sigma: an empirical analysis. *Total Quality Management and Business Excellence, 31*(3-4), 279-296.
[http://dx.doi.org/10.1080/14783363.2018.1426452]

Sarker, I. H. (2021). Data Science and Analytics: An Overview from Data-Driven Smart Computing, Decision-Making and Applications Perspective. *SN Computer Science 2,* 5, 377.
[http://dx.doi.org/10.1007/s42979-021-00765-8]

Saura, J.R., Ribeiro-Soriano, D., Palacios-Marqués, D. (2021). From user-generated data to data-driven innovation: A research agenda to understand user privacy in digital markets. *International Journal of Information Management., 60*, 102331.
[http://dx.doi.org/10.1016/j.ijinfomgt.2021.102331]

Schiff, D., Biddle, J., Borenstein, J., & Laas, K. (2020). What's next for AI ethics, policy, and governance? A global overview. *AIES 2020 - Proceedings of the AAAI/ACM Conference on AI, Ethics, and Society,* 153–158.
[http://dx.doi.org/10.1145/3375627.3375804]

Schildkamp, K. (2019). Data-based decision-making for school improvement: Research insights and gaps. *Educational Researcher, 61*(3), 257-273.
[http://dx.doi.org/10.1080/00131881.2019.1625716]

Schmitt, M. (2023). Automated machine learning: AI-driven decision making in business analytics. *Intelligent Systems with Applications, 18*, 200188.
[http://dx.doi.org/10.1016/j.iswa.2023.200188]

Schrettenbrunnner, M. B. (2020). Artificial-intelligence-driven management. *IEEE Engineering Management Review, 48,* 2, pp. 15-19. Available from: https://ieeexplore.ieee.org/abstract/document/9079641/.

Sharma, A., Sharma, A., Agarwal, A., Parween, S., Shrivastava, A., & Hajra, V. (2024). Artificial

Intelligence and business strategy towards digital transformation: A research agenda. *Nanotechnology Perceptions 20,* S6, pp. 46–58.
[http://dx.doi.org/10.62441/nano-ntp.v20iS6.5]

Sharma, M., Luthra, S., Joshi, S., Kumar, A. (2022). Implementing challenges of artificial intelligence: Evidence from public manufacturing sector of an emerging economy. *Government Information Quarterly, 39*(4), 101624.
[http://dx.doi.org/10.1016/j.giq.2021.101624]

Shaw, J., Rudzicz, F., Jamieson, T., & Goldfarb, A. (2019). Artificial Intelligence and the Implementation Challenge. *Journal of Medical Internet Research 21,* 7.
[http://dx.doi.org/10.2196/13659]

Sjödin, D., Parida, V., Palmié, M., Wincent, J. (2021). How AI capabilities enable business model innovation: Scaling AI through co-evolutionary processes and feedback loops. *Journal of Business Research, 134*, 574-587.
[http://dx.doi.org/10.1016/j.jbusres.2021.05.009]

Son, T.H., Weedon, Z., Yigitcanlar, T., Sanchez, T., Corchado, J.M., Mehmood, R. (2023). Algorithmic urban planning for smart and sustainable development: Systematic review of the literature. *Sustainable Cities and Society,* Elsevier.*4* , 104562.
[http://dx.doi.org/10.1016/j.scs.2023.104562]

Stone, M., Aravopoulou, E., Ekinci, Y., Evans, G., Hobbs, M., Labib, A., Laughlin, P., Machtynger, J., Machtynger, L. (2020). Artificial intelligence (AI) in strategic marketing decision-making: a research agenda. *Bottom Line, 33*(2), 183-200.
[http://dx.doi.org/10.1108/BL-03-2020-0022]

Strohm, L., Hehakaya, C., Ranschaert, E. R., Boon, W. P. C., & Moors, E. H. M. (2020). Implementation of artificial intelligence (AI) applications in radiology: hindering and facilitating factors. *European Radiology 30,* 10, pp. 5525–5532.
[http://dx.doi.org/10.1007/s00330-020-06946-y]

Tarafdar, M., Beath, C. M., & Ross, J. W. (2020). Using AI to Enhance Business Operations. *How AI is transforming the organization,* 67–86 .
[http://dx.doi.org/10.7551/mitpress/12588.003.0015]

Trabucchi, D., Buganza, T. (2019). Data-driven innovation: switching the perspective on Big Data. *European Journal of Innovation Management, 22*(1), 23-40.
[http://dx.doi.org/10.1108/EJIM-01-2018-0017]

Troisi, O., Maione, G., Grimaldi, M., Loia, F. (2020). Growth hacking: Insights on data-driven decision-making from three firms. *Industrial Marketing Management, 90*, 538-557.
[http://dx.doi.org/10.1016/j.indmarman.2019.08.005]

Usman, M., Khan, R., Moinuddin, M. (2024). Assessing the Impact of Artificial Intelligence Adoption on Organizational Performance in the Manufacturing Sector. *Revista Española de Documentación Científica, 18*(02), 95-116.

Usman, F.O., Eyo-Udo, N.L., Ayodeji Adegbola, , Etukudoh, E.A., Odonkor, B., Ibeh, C.V., Adegbola, A. (2024). A critical review of AI-driven strategies for entrepreneurial success. *International Journal of Management & Entrepreneurship Research, 6*(1), 200-215.
[http://dx.doi.org/10.51594/ijmer.v6i1.748]

Van Ooijen, C., Ubaldi, B., & Welby, B. (2019). A data-driven public sector: Enabling the strategic use of data for productive, inclusive and trustworthy governance (*OECD Working Papers on Public Governance* No. 33). OECD Publishing.
[http://dx.doi.org/10.1787/09ab162c-en]

Wamba-Taguimdje, S.L., Fosso Wamba, S., Kala Kamdjoug, J.R., Tchatchouang Wanko, C.E. (2020). Influence of artificial intelligence (AI) on firm performance: the business value of AI-based transformation projects. *Business Process Management Journal, 26*(7), 1893-1924.

[http://dx.doi.org/10.1108/BPMJ-10-2019-0411]

Wirtz, B.W., Weyerer, J.C., Geyer, C. (2019). Artificial Intelligence and the public sector—applications and challenges. *International Journal of Public Administration, 42*(7), 596-615.
[http://dx.doi.org/10.1080/01900692.2018.1498103]

Wu, C-J., Raghavendra, R., Gupta, U., Acun, B., Ardalani, N., Maeng, K., Chang, G., Aga, F., Huang, J., Bai, C., Gschwind, M., Gupta, A., Ott, M., Melnikov, A., Candido, S., Brooks, D., Chauhan, G., Lee, B., Lee, H-H., Akyildiz, B., Balandat, M., Spisak, J., Jain, R., Rabbat, M., & Hazelwood, K. Sustainable AI: Environmental implications, challenges and opportunities. *Proceedings of Machine Learning and Systems (MLSys).* Available from: https://proceedings.mlsys.org/paper_files/paper/2022/hash/462211f67c7d858f663355eff93b745e-Abstract.html.

Wu, C., Wu, P., Wang, J., Jiang, R., Chen, M., Wang, X. (2022). Critical review of data-driven decision-making in bridge operation and maintenance. *Structural Infrastructure Engineering, 18*(1), 47-70.
[http://dx.doi.org/10.1080/15732479.2020.1833946]

Yablonsky, S. A. (2019). Multidimensional data-driven artificial intelligence innovation. *Technology Innovation Management Review 9,* 12, pp. 16–28.
[http://dx.doi.org/10.22215/timreview/1288]

Yomboi, J., Majeed, M., & Asiedu, E. (2024). Product and the internet of things (IoT). *Disruptive Technologies and Business Innovation: IoT in Perspective,* 19–38. Available from: https://books.google.com/books?hl=en&lr=&id=k2A8EQAAQBAJ&oi=fnd&pg=PA19&dq=%22yomboi+jonas%22&ots=ApCh890Sbe&sig=m6OfkzcH7ocvvJNjFKivZHYJNTk.

Yomboi, J., Mohammed, M., Nangpiire, C., Nkayi, K., Gyau, E.K. and Manu, V.(2024). Utilizing technology for sustainable resource management solutions: Economics and finance. *Utilizing Technology for Sustainable Resource Management Solutions.* Available from: https://www.igi-global.com/chapter/utilizing-technolo-y-for-sustainable-resource-management-solutions/351193.
[http://dx.doi.org/10.4018/979-8-3693-2346-5.ch002]

CHAPTER 5

Optimizing AI in Resource Allocation

Abstract: This chapter explores the transformative role of Artificial Intelligence in enhancing organizational efficiency, productivity, and innovation. Through a review of relevant literature, case studies, and real-world examples, it examines AI's role in optimizing resource allocation, including time, talent, and capital. The findings indicate that AI significantly improves resource allocation by optimizing time management, talent deployment, and capital distribution. AI-driven scheduling and workflow automation enhance time efficiency, while predictive analytics improve recruitment, skill matching, and overall talent management. AI also enhances capital allocation by optimizing Return On Investment (ROI) and managing Operational (OpEx) and Capital Expenditures (CapEx) through data-driven insights. However, businesses must recognize the complexities of AI adoption and ensure proper integration into their operational strategies.

Keywords: AI, Business strategy, Capital, Data privacy, Ethical considerations, Operational efficiency, Sustainable growth.

INTRODUCTION

AI has rapidly transformed many industries, improving resource allocation, a key business success factor (Almansour, 2023). AI resource allocation strategically distributes time, talent, and capital (Bashynska *et al.*, 2023), that every company needs to compete. For years, businesses have used manual, human-driven resource allocation processes, which are inefficient, biased, and data-limited. AI's predictive insights and large dataset analysis improve resource allocation, efficiency, adaptability, and productivity (Almansour, 2023). Modern organizations need efficient resource management (Bashynska *et al.*, 2023). Companies are pressured to deliver high-quality goods and services cheaply and quickly. Resource allocation impacts innovation and market adaptability in project management, workforce optimization, and financial investments (Achchab and Temsamani, 2022). Inefficient resource allocation wastes resources, misses opportunities, and lowers returns, while optimized allocation improves decision-making, productivity, and organizational performance. AI automates redundant tasks, provides real-time insights, and enables data-driven strategic allocation (Aldulaimi *et al.*, 2021).

Resource allocation has always been important, but data-driven and complex industries have made resource management harder (Bashynska *et al.,* 2023). Modern organizations face resource allocation challenges like human capital management, financial asset distribution, and hourly productivity optimization. Organizations must efficiently allocate time, talent, and capital to compete globally. Incorrect allocation can cause bottlenecks, project delays, and financial losses (Allal-Chérif *et al.*, 2021). Conventional models allocate resources using historical data, intuition, and managerial skills (Bashynska *et al.*, 2023). Although beneficial, these methods are limited by human judgment and data analysis and interpretation. Data proliferation from enterprise digital transformation requires effective data management to maintain operational efficiency and innovate. Data processing and informed decision-making require AI (Almansour, 2023). AI improves resource allocation precision, velocity, and efficacy with machine learning, predictive analytics, and real-time data.

Organizations can meet deadlines, increase productivity, and cut costs by managing time when allocating resources (Almansour, 2023). AI automates repetitive tasks, optimizes workflow scheduling, and predicts project delays and inefficiencies. AI can update tasks in real-time, reallocate them based on employee workloads, and automate administrative tasks like meeting scheduling and report generation, freeing up human resources for strategic tasks (Alsaif & Aksoy, 2023). AI can predict future trends and outcomes from historical data. Anticipating time management delays lets companies reallocate resources before problems arise. AI tools in project management can identify workflow bottlenecks, suggest solutions, and adjust schedules to save time (Bashynska *et al.*, 2023). AI can coordinate many time-critical processes across departments or teams, ensuring each division works efficiently toward a goal.

AI greatly affects talent optimization and resource allocation. Organizations can gain a competitive edge by managing their most valuable asset, human resources (Bashynska *et al.*, 2023). AI-based HR systems improve recruitment by evaluating resumes, matching candidate qualifications to job specifications, and predicting employee performance. This reduces hiring time and improves talent (Berhil *et al.*, 2019). AI helps talent management by identifying skill gaps and suggesting reskilling or upskilling. AI can tailor development plans to future needs using performance metrics and employee data (Bian *et al.*, 2022). AI predicts future labor needs, helping businesses hire or train workers. AI talent optimization systems can predict turnover and employee sentiment (Chen *et al.*, 2022). AI can analyze employee surveys and feedback to assess engagement and retain top talent. Thus, AI boosts employee recruitment, retention, satisfaction, motivation, and productivity.

AI impacts capital allocation for projects, investments, and departments (Bashynska *et al.,* 2023). AI systems use predictive analytics to improve investment strategies, reduce risk, and make better financial decisions. These systems can evaluate real-time market data, project financial feasibility, and capital allocation for maximum ROI (Chima, 2022). AI predicts spending, finds cost-saving opportunities, and analyzes cash flow to improve budgeting. Additionally, it automates financial analysis, minimizes human error, accelerates decision-making, and channels capital toward high-growth sectors. This is especially advantageous in industries with tight profit margins, where financial errors can have significant consequences.

AI changes business operations, especially resource allocation. Resource allocation—distributing an organization's time, talent, and capital among competing projects or departments—determines operational efficiency and strategic goals (Afrin *et al.,* 2021). Human judgment, manual planning systems, and experience-based decision-making have allocated resources, but biases and limitations in processing large datasets can cause inefficiencies, delays, and suboptimal results (Agomuo *et al.,* 2024). Using advanced algorithms, machine learning models, and predictive analytics, AI optimizes resource use autonomously. Managing resources efficiently has long been key to organizational success. It impacts company goals, costs, and output. Human capital, financial investments, and time mismanagement can cause waste, inefficiency, and competitive disadvantage (Ahmed *et al.,* 2019). Organizations must adapt to market changes in today's fast-paced, technology-driven business environment, making resource allocation crucial. As AI technologies mature, organizations can analyze massive amounts of data, predict future demands, and allocate resources to reduce underutilization and overextension (Aldulaimi *et al.,* 2021).

Employees can focus on strategy while AI optimizes scheduling, automates routine tasks, and optimizes processes. AI can predict workflow bottlenecks, reassign tasks, and boost efficiency (Allal-Chérif *et al.,* 2021). AI-driven HR systems analyze resumes, match skills to job requirements, and predict employee performance to help companies hire and deploy the right talent (Almansour, 2023). AI finds skill gaps and recommends targeted upskilling or reskilling to keep the workforce competitive and aligned with strategic goals (Alsaif & Aksoy, 2023). AI drives capital allocation. AI-powered analytics and predictive modeling improve financial decisions. They forecast market trends, evaluate investment risks, and recommend project funding. Real-time data processing and actionable insights from AI help companies allocate capital for maximum ROI and minimum financial risk (Bashynska *et al.,* 2023). Business resilience and long-term success are improved by AI-powered capital allocation tools for budgeting, cash flow management, and financial planning. Time, talent, and capital are optimized by AI, revolutionizing resource allocation.

This chapter examines how AI improves efficiency, productivity, and innovation in organizational resource management. A review of relevant literature, case studies, and real-world examples will show how AI helps businesses allocate resources. The chapter also discusses organizations' challenges in adopting AI for resource optimization and future trends that may influence AI's role in resource management. Fig. (**1**) below provides a visual representation of the study's findings.

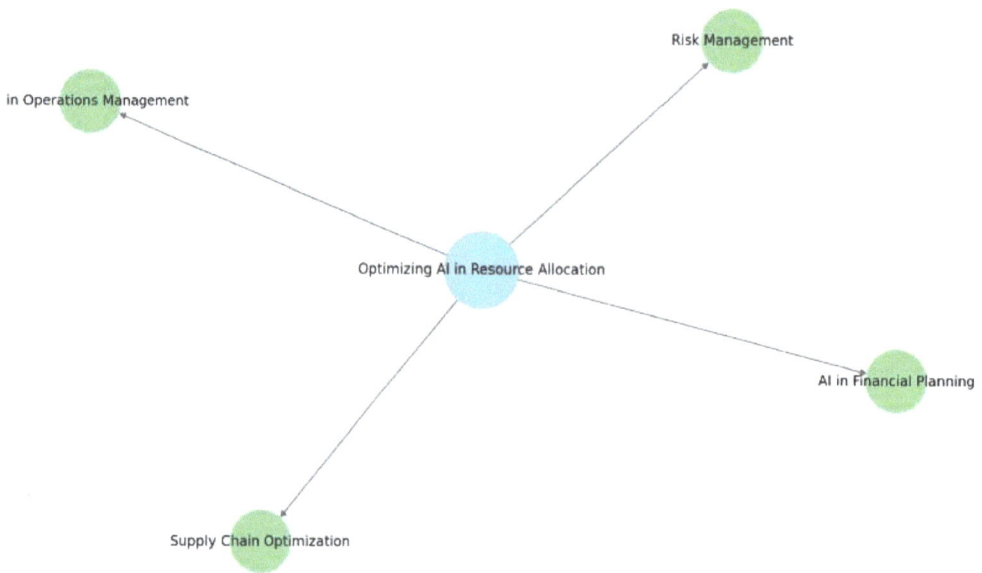

Fig. (1). Conceptual framework.

LITERATURE REVIEW

AI and Time Management

Organizational success requires time management (Amershi *et al.*, 2019). AI time management has improved business efficiency and competitiveness (Agomuo *et al.,* 2024). AI helps with automation, project management, and timekeeping. Companies also utilize AI to schedule strategic, goal-oriented activities.

Automation of Routine Tasks and its Effect on Time Allocation

One of AI's biggest contributions to time management is automating tedious tasks (Agomuo *et al.,* 2024). Data entry, meeting scheduling, and email management take up a lot of time, limiting strategic thinking (Amershi *et al.*, 2019). AI automates mundane tasks, freeing up employees to work on important projects. AI-powered email sorting tools help employees prioritize important messages over spam (Afrin *et al.,* 2021). Cortana and Assistant save employees time by scheduling meetings, sending reminders, and managing calendars (Agomuo *et al.*, 2024). Automation helps team members focus on core goals without being distracted by logistics, improving time management and collaboration.

AI Tools for Project Management and Time Tracking

AI time tracking and project management tools optimize time allocation. These tools use machine learning algorithms to show project timelines, resource utilization, and task dependencies to help teams allocate time. AI schedulers optimize meetings and tasks based on team members' availability, workload, and priorities. Schedule conflicts decrease, and team efficiency increases (Ahmed *et al.*, 2019). AI workflow automation tools assign tasks based on rules and performance data to simplify complex processes. This cuts time and task management errors (Aldulaimi *et al.*, 2021). Based on past data, Asana and Trello use AI to predict project completion times, helping managers allocate time and resources and adjust timelines. AI provides real-time project and task time analytics in time-tracking apps. Businesses use data to identify and improve inefficiencies. AI can identify slow, unproductive tasks, prompting strategy changes (Allal-Chérif *et al.*, 2021).

Case Studies Showing Improved Time Efficiency Through AI-driven Tools

Many case studies showed that AI improves organizational time management and efficiency. AI-driven project management improved IBM's collaboration and workflows. IBM analyzed project data and team dynamics with AI algorithms to find bottlenecks and optimize department resources. Project completion and productivity increased significantly (Almansour, 2023). AI-based scheduling software optimized shifts and store time for another large retailer. The AI system optimized schedules to match labor resources to peak demand using historical sales data, employee availability, and customer traffic patterns. Employee satisfaction and peak-hour sales increased by 20% due to work-life balance (Alsaif & Aksoy, 2023). Software Company tracked developers' project time with AI. Understanding productivity patterns and slow tasks helped the company allocate resources and reduce project delays. This balanced the team workload and increased project throughput by 30% (Amershi *et al.,* 2019). AI-integrated time management changes how companies use their most valuable resource—time. AI automates routine tasks, improves project management, and tracks time to maximize productivity and business results. AI will improve time management, helping companies adapt to changing business conditions.

AI in Talent Management

The ever-changing business landscape makes talent management essential. Optimizing talent management processes can give companies an edge because human capital is their most valuable asset. AI has transformed talent management by improving recruitment, skill assessment, performance management, and employee engagement. This section highlights AI's achievements in recruitment, skill matching, performance prediction, and implementation.

AI's Role in Recruitment and Human Resource Allocation

HR-critical recruitment has changed with AI. Inefficient and biased candidate selection results from manual labor in traditional recruitment. AI-powered recruitment tools streamline hiring by screening resumes, candidates, and job descriptions. AI can quickly screen thousands of applications for the best skills, experience, and culture fit (Albert, 2019). Chatbots and virtual assistants can improve recruitment by reaching candidates live. These tools answer questions, schedule interviews, and update applications, improving candidate experience. AI-based hiring can cut time-to-hire by 50%, allowing HR teams to focus on strategic projects, according to Afrin *et al.* (2021). HR allocation can be improved by AI analyzing workforce data and predicting staffing demand. This predictive capability optimizes workforce allocation to meet corporate needs with the right talent at the right time (Agomuo *et al.*, 2024).

Predictive Analytics in Employee Performance Management

Another powerful AI talent management tool for employee performance is predictive analytics. AI can help managers improve performance and employee development by analyzing historical performance data, employee behaviors, and external factors. AI can spot performance decline and disengagement, letting managers act before issues arise (Aldulaimi *et al.*, 2021). AI-driven performance management systems encourage continuous improvement with real-time feedback and coaching. These systems evaluate performance against predefined metrics and recommend development plans based on strengths and weaknesses. AI performance management increased employee productivity and teamwork by 25% at a technology company (Allal-Chérif *et al.*, 2021).

Case Studies of Companies Successfully Using AI for Talent Optimization

AI has improved talent acquisition, performance management, and employee engagement in many companies. Unilever evaluates candidates' cognitive skills using AI and gamified assessments. This shorter hiring process increases talent diversity and candidate satisfaction (Almansour, 2023). AI and predictive analytics improve performance management at Deloitte. Based on employee reviews and feedback, Deloitte's dynamic performance management system recommends personalized coaching and development. Employee satisfaction and retention improve with AI talent management (Alsaif & Aksoy, 2023). Walmart plans talent with AI. Walmart allocates staff based on customer demand and sales patterns using predictive analytics, reducing labour costs and improving service (Amershi *et al.*, 2019). AI enhances talent management by improving recruitment, skill matching, and performance management. AI enhances talent management, resource allocation, employee engagement, and organizational performance. Talent management will improve with AI, giving companies more ways to use human capital.

AI in Capital Allocation

Capital allocation maximizes returns and meets goals in business strategy. Financial market complexity and data abundance make traditional capital allocation methods ineffective. AI-enhanced analytical and predictive tools are changing capital allocation. AI tools, investment optimization, and real-world case studies of AI-driven capital management's financial impact are covered here (Achchab and Temsamani, 2022).

Overview of AI Applications in Financial Decision-making

Financial decision-making uses AI for risk assessment, portfolio management, fraud detection, and compliance. Companies use machine learning algorithms to find patterns, predict outcomes, and optimize investment strategies in large datasets. Acharya and Arnold (2019) found that AI-driven technologies can boost financial institutions' decision-making speed and accuracy by 60%, helping them adapt to market changes. AI can measure capital allocation using real-time market trends, economic indicators, and historical performance. Financial analysts can make informed decisions using comprehensive insights rather than intuition or historical data (Achchab and Temsamani, 2022). AI can assess investment risks and returns to help companies allocate capital.

AI for Investment Optimization

Predicting Return On Investment (ROI) and Guiding CapEx and OpEx Decisions

AI optimizes CapEx and OpEx and predicts ROI. AI predicts investment returns using past performance and market trends. Data-driven financial decisions require prediction. By analyzing cash flows, expenses, and risks, AI can help businesses allocate project resources. This helps capital-intensive industries that invest in technology and infrastructure. AI investment optimization increased ROI by 10–15% over conventional methods. AI can identify CapEx and OpEx cost-saving opportunities. AI systems analyze operational data to cut costs without compromising quality or service (Agomuo *et al*., 2024). This lets firms prioritize high-return investments.

Examples and Case Studies on the Financial Impact of AI-driven Capital Management

Many AI tools aid financial planning and capital allocation. Robo-advisors match investment portfolios to risk tolerance and financial goals using algorithms. These platforms analyzed market conditions, portfolio rebalancing, and personalized investment advice without human intervention. AI-driven financial management solutions will grow the global robo-advisory market to $2.5 trillion by 2025, according to Ahmed *et al.* (2019). AI-powered financial planning tools alter capital allocation. Personal financial data and machine learning algorithms suggest budgeting, saving, and investing. Real-time spending insights and personalized advice from Cleo and YNAB (You Need A Budget) help manage finances (Ai and Bhandari, 2021). AI-driven analytics platforms like Tableau and Qlik help decision-makers identify trends and allocate capital by visualizing and interpreting complex financial data (Li *et al*., 2020). These tools help financial teams evaluate risks, simulate "what-if" scenarios, and predict performance, improving capital management.

Many firms have benefited from AI-driven capital management. Major asset manager BlackRock uses AI to improve portfolio performance and decision-making. After using AI to analyze massive amounts of data, BlackRock improved its investment strategies and increased assets under management by over $1 trillion (Yang, 2023). Siemens uses AI to optimize capital allocation for projects. Siemens used predictive analytics to assess ROI and cut project costs by €1 billion (Albert, 2019). AI capital allocation improves financial performance in this example. AI helps Square and other fintechs lend and process payments. Square grows its lending portfolio and lowers default rates by using machine learning algorithms to assess credit risk and predict loan defaults. This enhances capital allocation and customer satisfaction (Aldulaimi *et al.*, 2021). Advances in AI improve financial decision-making, revolutionizing capital allocation. Predictive analytics, AI, and case studies can boost investment strategies and profits. AI's capital management role will grow as technology improves, helping organizations maximize finances.

AI-driven Decision-making in Resource Allocation

AI-based resource allocation has changed industry decision-making. AI technologies like machine learning, predictive analytics, and optimization algorithms help organizations optimize efficiency and effectiveness and make better decisions. AI systems that improve complex decision-making, real-time data processing for dynamic allocation, and intelligent resource allocation are discussed in this section.

The Role of Machine Learning, Predictive Analytics, and Optimization Algorithms in Decision-making

Machine learning improves AI without programming by learning from data. From historical data, machine learning algorithms predict future needs and allocate resources. Companies can avoid stockouts by allocating inventory using machine learning algorithms to predict supply chain demand (Acharya and Arnold, 2019). Statistics and machine learning improve decision-making in predictive analytics. Predicting future outcomes helps organizations allocate resources. Patient flow can be used to allocate staff and resources in hospitals using predictive analytics (Achchab and Temsamani, 2022). Proactive resource optimization improves operations and patient care. Constrained resource allocation is optimized by algorithms. Optimization algorithms evaluate multiple variables and constraints to maximize outputs or minimize costs. Portfolio optimization algorithms help finance investors maximize returns and minimize risk (Afrin *et al.*, 2021). Companies make data-driven strategic decisions using these algorithms.

Real-time Data Processing for Dynamic Resource Allocation

Real-time data processing changes resource allocation, enabling quick adaptation. Analyzing new data helps businesses make faster, more flexible decisions. Real-time production line data helps manufacturers allocate maintenance resources and reduce downtime (Agomuo *et al.*, 2024). Real-time shipment and inventory tracking optimizes logistics chains. AI systems can reroute delivery vehicles and allocate resources, reducing delays and costs (Ahmed *et al.*, 2019). Delivering on time with dynamic resource allocation improves operational efficiency and customer satisfaction. Real-time data improves workforce management and resource allocation. AI-driven scheduling tools let managers deploy talent based on real-time employee availability, skills, and project needs (Ai and Bhandari, 2021). The dynamic approach lets organizations optimize employee use and adapt to project needs.

Multiple AI systems improved complex resource allocation. Watson from IBM uses AI and machine learning to provide industry insights. Watson may recommend treatments, optimize resource allocation, and improve healthcare (Li *et al.*, 2020). Healthcare providers can match staff, equipment, and facilities to patients. BlackRock manages portfolios and invests with AI. Aladdin uses machine learning and predictive analytics to analyze market data, assess risks, and optimize asset allocations across asset classes at BlackRock. This system helps financial professionals make risk-adjusted investment decisions that meet goals (Yang, 2023). Amazon optimizes inventory and delivery routes with AI-powered logistics and supply chain management using predictive analytics and real-time data processing. Amazon meets customer demand by analyzing historical sales, market trends, and real-time order data (Bankins, 2021). Customer service and operational efficiency improve with Amazon's optimization. Organizations are changing resource management due to AI allocation. Machine learning, predictive analytics, and optimization algorithms improve business decisions and resource allocation. Companies can adjust resources with real-time data processing. Implementation in various industries shows that AI systems can transform resource allocation and drive organizational success.

CHALLENGES IN AI-BASED RESOURCE ALLOCATION

AI resource allocation has pros and cons. To implement AI-driven resource management systems, organizations must overcome ethical, data quality, and internal barriers. AI model ethics, data quality, bias, and organizational barriers to AI-based resource allocation are covered here.

Ethics matter when allocating AI resources. Ethical AI requires fairness, transparency, and accountability. Fair AI algorithms must not discriminate in resource distribution. Firms creating AI systems must avoid biases that hurt marginalized groups. These issues can damage reputation, legal issues, and stakeholder trust if ignored (Abedi and Pourkiani, 2020). Another moral issue is transparency. Stakeholders must understand AI-driven resource allocation. Clear algorithm and data explanations are needed. Without transparency, organizations risk alienating stakeholders and being judged for AI fairness (Bashynska *et al.*, 2023). Trust and accountability in AI-driven resource allocation require ethics, fairness, and transparency.

Data quality hinders AI resource allocation. AI systems trained on flawed or biased data will produce inaccurate and potentially harmful results. An AI model trained on historical data showing systemic biases like underrepresentation can perpetuate resource allocation discrimination (Bega *et al.*, 2020). Companies must prioritize high-quality, representative data collection and curation to reduce AI model bias and ensure fair outcomes. AI systems require constant data updates due to dynamic resource allocation. Good data management keeps AI model data current, relevant, and accurate. It takes multiple data sources and validation, and verification (Berhil *et al.*, 2019). AI-driven resource allocation benefits from data quality.

Organizational Challenges to AI Adoption in Resource Allocation

Companies allocating resources with AI face ethical, data quality, and internal issues. Culture, technology, and structure can hinder AI system integration. Employees may fear job loss or doubt AI's abilities due to cultural resistance to change. Organizations must emphasize AI's collaborative potential and support for human decision-making to overcome this resistance (Bian *et al.*, 2022). Structures hinder AI adoption. Many companies lack AI processes and infrastructure. AI may not fit workflows, causing inefficiency and employee frustration (Bilen *et al.*, 2022). Organizations need AI technology and training to allocate resources. Data silos and system interoperability hinder AI adoption. Organizations must link data sources and systems to optimize AI resource allocation. Eliminating data silos, standardising formats, and using integrated platforms can improve data flow (Ilager *et al.*, 2020). AI optimizes resource allocation, but organizations face many challenges. Ethics, data quality, and organizational barriers must be considered when using AI for resource management. AI can improve fair, transparent, data-integrated organizational resource allocation.

Case Studies and Industry Applications of AI in Resource Allocation

AI impacts industry and resource allocation. Time, talent, and capital optimization boost productivity. Case studies in healthcare, manufacturing, and finance show how AI improves resource management and delivers valuable lessons. Healthcare scheduling, management, and resource use benefit from AI. The Mount Sinai Health System in New York improved operating room scheduling with AI. Historical data, patient conditions, and surgeon availability optimize schedules. Mount Sinai's operating room efficiency increased by 20%, reducing patient wait times (Ahmad *et al.*, 2021).

Key Success Factors:

- **Data Utilization**: Using historical data and real-time analytics enabled the development of precise scheduling algorithms that adapt to varying demands.

- **Cross-disciplinary Collaboration**: The project required close collaboration among healthcare professionals, data scientists, and IT specialists, ensuring the AI tool addressed the specific needs of medical staff.
- **Continuous Learning**: The AI system is designed to learn from ongoing operations, allowing for iterative improvements in scheduling algorithms based on new data and changing circumstances.

Lessons Learned:

- **Stakeholder Buy-in**: Gaining the support of medical staff and administration was crucial for successful implementation. Engaging stakeholders in the development process fostered a sense of ownership and trust in the AI system.
- **Scalability**: Developing AI solutions that can scale across different departments within the healthcare facility enhances overall resource optimization and allows for a more unified approach to patient care.

AI in Manufacturing: Streamlining Operations

Manufacturing companies use AI to optimize their supply chain and production. Siemens' factory AI-driven predictive maintenance solutions are an example. Siemens predicts equipment failures from machinery and production line data, reducing downtime and enabling timely maintenance. The proactive approach has reduced unplanned downtime by 30%, improving production efficiency (Acharya and Arnold, 2019).

Key Success Factors:

- **Real-time Monitoring**: Continuous data collection from machinery facilitated real-time analytics and predictive modeling, which are vital for effective maintenance scheduling.
- **Integration with Existing Systems**: The AI solution was integrated with Siemens' existing Enterprise Resource Planning (ERP) systems, allowing seamless data sharing and comprehensive analysis.
- **Employee Training**: Siemens invested in training its workforce to understand and leverage AI insights effectively, empowering employees to engage with new technologies confidently.

Lessons Learned:

- **Iterative Implementation**: Adopting a phased approach allowed Siemens to refine its AI models based on feedback and performance data, minimizing risks associated with abrupt changes.

- **Data Security**: Ensuring the security of sensitive operational data was essential for maintaining trust among stakeholders and complying with regulatory standards.

AI in Finance: Enhancing Decision-making

Finance, capital allocation, and risk management have changed with AI. For investment decisions, JPMorgan Chase uses AI algorithms to analyze massive financial data and market trends. AI-powered LOXM executes trades at optimal prices, improving efficiency and reducing trading costs by 30% (Achchab & Temsamani, 2022).

Key Success Factors:

- **Algorithm Development**: A robust development process focused on creating sophisticated algorithms capable of processing complex financial data efficiently.
- **Real-time Analytics**: Access to real-time data enables the organization to respond quickly to market fluctuations and optimize investment decisions.
- **Regulatory Compliance**: Prioritizing compliance with regulatory standards minimizes the risk of non-compliance, ensuring the responsible use of AI in trading.

Lessons Learned:

- **Transparency in AI**: Providing transparency in algorithmic decision-making fosters trust among stakeholders and clients, which is critical in the financial sector.
- **Ethical Considerations**: Addressing potential biases in trading algorithms was essential to maintain fairness and avoid regulatory scrutiny, thereby supporting ethical practices in financial services.

These case studies demonstrate AI resource allocation across industries. Data, cross-disciplinary collaboration, and learning have helped these organizations succeed. These implementations demonstrate that AI adoption requires stakeholder buy-in, scalability, and transparency. The AI application insights will help organizations optimize time, talent, and capital with innovative technologies.

FUTURE TRENDS IN AI AND RESOURCE ALLOCATION

As organizations embrace AI's transformative power, several new technologies will affect resource allocation. Time, talent, and capital management innovations are led by reinforcement learning and quantum computing (Abdeldayem and Aldulaimi, 2020). These emerging technologies, AI's resource optimization future, and strategic resource allocation are discussed. Reinforcement learning changes how companies allocate resources. RL improves decision-making with environmental feedback and trial-and-error learning (Abedi and Pourkiani, 2020). Due to its adaptability, RL can optimize supply chain management and project scheduling (Acharya and Arnold, 2019). Real-time data-driven resource allocation boosts efficiency and results.

Another innovative resource allocation technology is quantum computing. Quantum mechanics lets quantum computers analyze massive datasets and solve complex optimization problems at unprecedented speeds (Afrin *et al.*, 2021). Quantum computing may improve logistics and investment resource allocation. Advances in AI can predict resource allocation optimization. Companies can efficiently allocate resources with AI. Reduced manual interventions will help businesses adapt faster to demand and resource changes. Advanced analytics and AI help organizations predict resource needs. AI systems can predict demand from historical data and market trends to help businesses allocate resources.

Resource allocation can be customized with advanced AI (Deng *et al.*, 2020). Using patient needs and historical treatment outcomes, AI can allocate medical staff and equipment to improve care and resource utilization. Future AI may help humans allocate resources. These systems will help organizations make informed decisions with human input by providing insights and recommendations. Strategic resource allocation is changing rapidly as organizations realize AI can improve decision-making and efficiency. AI helps companies plan long-term resources. Aligned resources support organizational goals. AI will optimize resource allocation for environmental impact as companies prioritize sustainability. Through waste reduction, energy optimization, and supply chain optimization, AI can help organizations allocate resources sustainably. AI resource allocation without industry bias. Healthcare, manufacturing, and finance use AI to optimize resource management. AI improves resource allocation across industries, demonstrating its versatility and efficacy. Continuous learning may help future AI systems adapt to new information and circumstances. Adaptability improves resource allocation, keeping organizations agile and market-responsive.

CONCLUSION

This literature review found that AI optimizes time, talent, and capital in resource allocation across organizations. AI's time, talent, and capital allocation applications show its strategic resource management value. AI streamlines timekeeping. Teams can better manage time with AI schedulers and workflow automation. With predictive analytics, AI can improve recruitment, skill matching, and talent management performance. AI capital allocation optimizes

ROI and manages OpEx and CapEx using data. These findings matter for business. Organizations considering AI for resource optimization must first understand its many uses. They should purchase and train staff to use strategic AI tools. Businesses should promote AI-integrated daily operations to help humans and AI systems collaborate. To maximize AI's resource allocation, several areas should be researched and developed. AI-driven resource management ethics must include fairness, transparency, and accountability in automated decision-making. Study AI's long-term effects on workforce dynamics, especially job displacement and work change. As AI technologies advance, research should improve algorithms and machine learning to solve complex resource allocation problems across industries. Quantum computing and reinforcement learning in resource management are intriguing.

REFERENCES

Abdeldayem, M. M., & Aldulaimi, S. H. (2020). Trends and opportunities of artificial intelligence in human resource management: Aspirations for public sector in Bahrain. *International Journal of Scientific and Technology Research 9,* 1, pp. 3867–3871. academia.edu. Available from: https://www.academia.edu/download/75869495/Trends-And-Opportunities-Of-Artificial-Intelligence-In-Human-Resource-Management-Aspirations-For-Public-Sector-In-Bahrain.pdf.

Abedi, M., & Pourkiani, M. (2020). Resource allocation in combined fog-cloud scenarios by using Artificial Intelligence *5th International Conference on Fog and Mobile Edge Computing*, FMEC 2020, 218–222. [http://dx.doi.org/10.1109/FMEC49853.2020.9144693]

Acharya, A., & Arnold, Z. (2019). Chinese Public AI R&D Spending: Provisional Findings CSET Issue Brief. Chinese public AI R&D spending: Provisional findings. *CSET Issue Brief.* pp. 1–31. pdfs.semanticscholar.org.   Available   from: https://pdfs.semanticscholar.org/d370/e67851e2c235ed7d14d964b6fee4633b7a6b.pdf.

Achchab, S., Temsamani, Y.K. (2022). Use of Artificial Intelligence in human resource management: Application of machine learning algorithms to an Intelligent recruitment system". *Lecture Notes in Networks and Systems, 249*, 203-215. [http://dx.doi.org/10.1007/978-3-030-85365-5_20]

Afrin, M., Jin, J., Rahman, A., Rahman, A., Wan, J., Hossain, E. (2021). Resource allocation and service provisioning in multi-agent cloud robotics: A comprehensive survey. *IEEE Communications Surveys and Tutorials, 23*(2), 842-870. [http://dx.doi.org/10.1109/COMST.2021.3061435]

Agomuo, O.C., Brempong Jnr, O., Muzamal, J.H. (2024). Energy-aware AI-based optimal cloud infra allocation for provisioning of resources. *27th IEEE/ACIS International Summer Conference on Software Engineering Artificial Intelligence Networking and Parallel/Distributed Computing, SNPD 2024 - Proceedings,* 269-274. [http://dx.doi.org/10.1109/SNPD61259.2024.10673918]

Ahmad, T., Zhang, D., Huang, C., Zhang, H., Dai, N., Song, Y., Chen, H. (2021). Artificial Intelligence in sustainable energy industry: Status Quo, challenges and opportunities. *Journal of Cleaner Production, 289,* 125834. [http://dx.doi.org/10.1016/j.jclepro.2021.125834]

Ahmed, K.I., Tabassum, H., Hossain, E. (2019). Deep learning for radio resource allocation in multi-cell networks. *IEEE Network., 33*(6), 188-195. [http://dx.doi.org/10.1109/MNET.2019.1900029]

Albert, E.T. (2019). AI in talent acquisition: a review of AI-applications used in recruitment and selection.

Strategic HR Review, 18(5), 215-221.
[http://dx.doi.org/10.1108/SHR-04-2019-0024]

Aldulaimi, S.H., Abdeldayem, M.M., Mowafak, B.M., Abdulaziz, M.M. (2021). Experimental perspective of artificial intelligence technology in human resources management. *Applications of Artificial Intelligence in Business, Education and Healthcare, 954*, 487-511.
[http://dx.doi.org/10.1007/978-3-030-72080-3_26]

Allal-Chérif, O., Yela Aránega, A., Castaño Sánchez, R. (2021). Intelligent recruitment: How to identify, select, and retain talents from around the world using artificial intelligence. *Technological Forecasting and Social Change, 169*, 120822.
[http://dx.doi.org/10.1016/j.techfore.2021.120822]

Almansour, M. (2023). Artificial intelligence and resource optimization: A study of Fintech start-ups. *Resources Policy, 80*, 103250.
[http://dx.doi.org/10.1016/j.resourpol.2022.103250]

Alsaif, A., Sabih Aksoy, M. (2023). AI-HRM: Artificial Intelligence in human resource management: A literature review *Journal of Computing and Communication, 2*(2), 1-7.
[http://dx.doi.org/10.21608/jocc.2023.307053]

Amershi, S., Weld, D., Vorvoreanu, M., Fourney, A., Nushi, B., Collisson, P., Suh, J., Iqbal, S., Bennett, P.N., Inkpen, K., Teevan, J., Kikin-Gil, R., Horvitz, E. (2019). Guidelines for human-AI interaction. *Conference on Human Factors in Computing Systems - Proceedings.*
[http://dx.doi.org/10.1145/3290605.3300233]

Bankins, S. (2021). The ethical use of artificial intelligence in human resource management: a decision-making framework. *Ethics and Information Technology, 23*(4), 841-854.
[http://dx.doi.org/10.1007/s10676-021-09619-6]

Bashynska, I., Prokopenko, O., & Sala, D. (2023). Managing Human Capital with AI: Synergy of Talent and Technology. *ASEJ - Scientific Journal of Bielsko-Biala School of Finance and Law 27,* 3, pp. 39–45.
[http://dx.doi.org/10.19192/wsfip.sj3.2023.5]

Bega, D., Gramaglia, M., Garcia-Saavedra, A., Fiore, M., Banchs, A., Costa-Perez, X. (2020). Network slicing meets artificial intelligence: An AI-based framework for slice management. *IEEE Communications Magazine, 58*(6), 32-38.
[http://dx.doi.org/10.1109/MCOM.001.1900653]

Berhil, S., Benlahmar, H., & Labani, N. (2019). A review paper on artificial intelligence at the service of human resources management. *Indonesian Journal of Electrical Engineering and Computer Science 18,* 1, pp. 32–40. academia.edu.
[http://dx.doi.org/10.11591/ijeecs.v18.i1.pp32-40]

Bian, Y. jie, Xie, L., & Li, J. qi. (2022). Research on influencing factors of artificial intelligence multi-cloud scheduling applied talent training based on DEMATEL-TAISM. *Journal of Cloud Computing 11,* 1.
[http://dx.doi.org/10.1186/s13677-022-00315-4]

Bilen, T., Canberk, B., Sharma, V., Fahim, M., & Duong, T. Q. (2022). AI-Driven Aeronautical Ad Hoc Networks for 6G Wireless: Challenges, Opportunities, and the Road Ahead. *Sensors 22,* 10, 3731. mdpi.com..
[http://dx.doi.org/10.3390/s22103731]

Chen, C.C., Wei, C.C., Chen, S.H., Sun, L.M., Lin, H.H. (2022). AI predicted competency model to maximize job performance. *Cybernetics and Systems, 53*(3), 298-317.
[http://dx.doi.org/10.1080/01969722.2021.1983701]

Deng, S., Zhao, H., Fang, W., Yin, J., Dustdar, S., Zomaya, A.Y. (2020). Edge Intelligence: The confluence of edge computing and artificial intelligence. *IEEE Internet of Things Journal, 7*(8), 7457-7469.
[http://dx.doi.org/10.1109/JIOT.2020.2984887]

Hussain, F., Hassan, S.A., Hussain, R., Hossain, E. (2020). Machine Learning for resource management in

cellular and iot networks: Potentials, current solutions, and open challenges. *IEEE Communications Surveys and Tutorials, 22*(2), 1251-1275.
[http://dx.doi.org/10.1109/COMST.2020.2964534]

Ilager, S., Muralidhar, R., Buyya, R. (2020). Artificial intelligence (AI)-centric management of resources in modern distributed computing systems. *Proceedings - 2020 IEEE Cloud Summit, Cloud Summit, 2020*, 1-10.
[http://dx.doi.org/10.1109/IEEECloudSummit48914.2020.00007]

Li, J., Carayon, P. (2021). Health Care 4.0: A vision for smart and connected health care. *IISE Transactions on Healthcare Systems Engineering, 11*(3), 1-10.
[http://dx.doi.org/10.1080/24725579.2021.1884627] [PMID: 34497970]

Yang, L. (2023). Firms' socially responsible activities: the role of the Big Three. *Journal of Economics and Finance, 47*(4), 859-883.
[http://dx.doi.org/10.1007/s12197-023-09622-1]

CHAPTER 6

AI in Resource Allocation: Optimizing Time, Talent, and Capital

Abstract: This chapter explores the role of Artificial Intelligence (AI) in optimizing resource allocation and its implications for improving organizational performance. The findings indicate that AI significantly improves resource allocation by automating routine tasks, optimizing recruitment strategies, and enhancing financial decision-making. AI-powered tools for time management increase scheduling efficiency and reduce idle time, while AI-driven human resource management improves talent acquisition, skill identification, and employee development. In capital management, AI enhances financial forecasting, investment decisions, and overall financial reporting accuracy. However, AI implementation also presents challenges, such as data security risks, algorithmic biases, and concerns over the potential dehumanization of roles. Despite these obstacles, ongoing technological advancements and careful implementation can mitigate these challenges, ensuring AI's effectiveness in resource optimization.

Keywords: AI, Capital, Organizational performance, Technological aspect, Time, Talent.

INTRODUCTION

In the context of technological progress and educational evolution, the intersection of talent management and AI tools has become a central concern in industrial sectors. This convergence offers promising opportunities to revolutionize methods for recognizing and cultivating academic skills within industrial settings. In today's business management landscape, the strategic deployment of resources, including time, talent, and capital, is crucial for success. As organizations seek to enhance their efficiency and effectiveness, incorporating AI into resource allocation processes emerges as a game-changing approach. AI technologies, known for their capacity to examine extensive datasets, recognize patterns, and generate valuable insights, have transformed traditional resource allocation models.

AI has recently emerged as a significant force in human resources, reshaping various aspects of HR management. Its impact spans key areas, such as recruitment training, development, and employee retention, altering conventional HR practices and dynamics. The transformative influence of AI has been substantial, underscoring its importance in modern HR environments (Khan *et al.*, 2024). Bhagyalakshmi and Maria (2021) highlighted the vital role of AI in Human Resource Management (HRM), noting its considerable contribution to maximizing human resource potential and boosting overall organizational efficacy. The potential of AI in talent management presents an encouraging outlook for companies' futures, creating new opportunities to tackle institutional challenges in enhancing corporate skills.

The combination of talent management, which concentrates on identifying, attracting, and retaining exceptional workplace talent with AI technologies, offers transformative possibilities through AI analytics, predictive modeling, and learning algorithms (Briki *et al.*, 2024). This enables companies to streamline and improve talent identification processes. Furthermore, utilizing AI in talent development delivers highly personalized experiences, adaptive training modules, and initiatives that target skill enhancement tailored to the diverse needs and aspirations of industrial professionals, making them feel valued and accommodated. AI provides features to automate routine tasks with exceptional intelligence, efficiency, and effectiveness, ensuring compliance and error detection while suggesting suitable adjustments and tools for workflow management. These procedures and interfaces guide HR specialists in boosting productivity and efficiency by automating repetitive tasks, proposing intelligent measures to address them, and offering appropriate solutions (Briki *et al.*, 2024). They also automate date, time, and expense entries and provide compensation packages for hiring managers to new employees.

This chapter investigates the role of AI in optimizing resource allocation, emphasizing its implications for improving organizational performance. We aim to explore how AI applications can streamline operations, minimize waste, and enhance decision-making across various sectors. By examining current literature, we uncover the intricacies of AI-driven resource allocation, focusing on three key aspects: time optimization, talent management, and capital allocation. Additionally, it addresses the challenges organizations face when implementing AI solutions and explores future trends that may shape the landscape of resource management. Fig. (**1**) illustrates the visual representation of the study's findings.

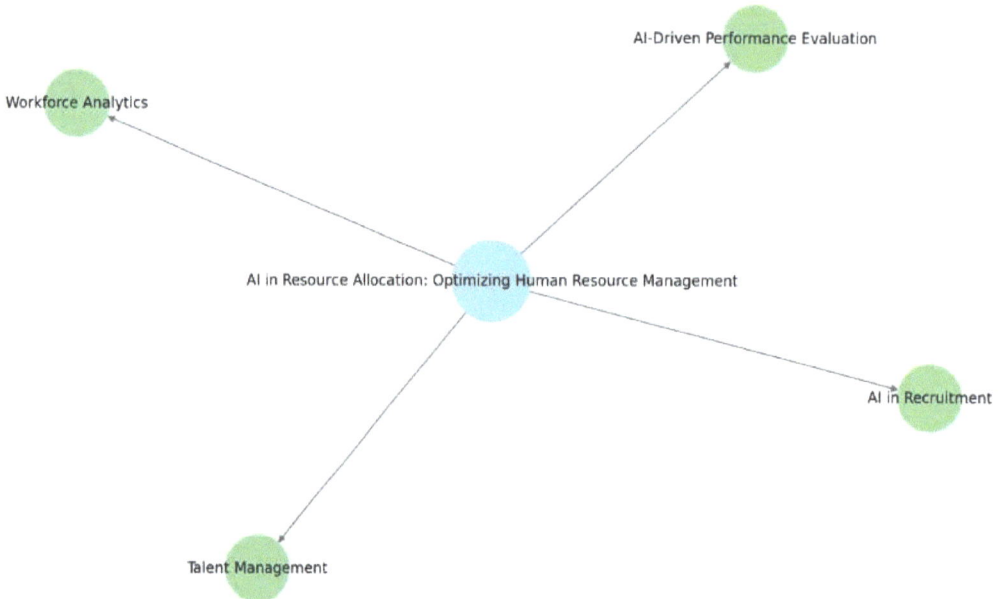

Fig. (1). Conceptual framework.

LITERATURE

AI in Resource Allocation

The emergence of Artificial Intelligence has transformed organizational approaches to resource allocation. Contemporary research highlights the ways in which AI enhances decision-making, particularly in optimizing resource distribution through real-time data analysis. AI-powered algorithms can evaluate operational metrics to efficiently allocate resources, leading to increased productivity.

Time Optimization

Effective time management is crucial for organizational success. AI-based tools can examine workflows and detect bottlenecks, thereby enabling improved scheduling and task assignment. For example, a study examined how AI-driven scheduling systems can substantially decrease downtime by anticipating and averting potential delays.

Talent Management

AI is increasingly shaping human resource management (HRM). Technologies, such as predictive analytics and machine learning, assist in identifying skill gaps and developing talent acquisition strategies. Research indicates that AI can improve recruitment processes by examining candidate information, allowing organizations to make more informed hiring choices.

Capital Allocation

Strategic investment decisions that drive organizational growth are central to capital allocations. AI models can predict financial trends, assess investment risks, and assist organizations in making data-driven capital allocation decisions. Studies (Asiedu *et al*., 2024; Charles *et al*., 2023; and Majeed *et al*., 2024; Yomboi *et al*., 2024) demonstrated the use of AI to enhance portfolio management, ultimately resulting in improved investment returns.

ADVANTAGES OF EFFICIENT RESOURCE DISTRIBUTION

While achieving optimal resource distribution can be challenging, when executed properly, it yields numerous advantages. The primary benefits include:

Employee Retention

Inadequate resource allocation can lead to workforce exhaustion. A poll conducted by CABA, an accountancy welfare organization, involving 1,222 UK accountants and ACA students, revealed that 40% of accountants experienced emotional exhaustion from their work. When questioned about the source of their stress, 33% identified their work, career, or studies as the primary cause. Organizations can enhance resource utilization, employee contentment, and retention through an effective resource allocation system. A well-designed allocation process optimizes utilization rates without overwhelming staff members. It also prevents overlooking other capable and available resources, ensuring fair and strategic task assignment. Moreover, by considering individual preferences, interests, and career goals during work allocation, companies can better support professional growth and retention.

Customer Satisfaction

Resource managers primarily focus on providing clients with the most suitable teams, blending industry expertise with appropriate skills and certifications to maximize quality and efficiency. While "best" is subjective, clients expect individuals with suitable qualifications and experience to be assigned to their projects. This includes people with relevant skills, insights, and knowledge specific to the client's business and industry. These may encompass technical abilities, sector experience, and essential soft skills. However, these competencies need not be concentrated in a single individual, location, or time zone. An optimal resource allocation system considers these factors and identifies a team with the most appropriate skills for each project phase. A resource management system that effectively utilizes personnel benefits both staff and client satisfaction.

Lucrative Engagements

Allocating the ideal resource combinations for complex projects requires comprehensive, current knowledge of resources' skills, capacity, and availability. It also necessitates the ability to accurately forecast the impact of resourcing decisions on engagement performance. In the long run, an effective allocation strategy helps organizations maintain a balance between over- and under-utilization of resources. This equilibrium reduces the risk of overburdening teams or overspending on unnecessary resources. Assigning the right resources to the appropriate engagement at the correct time enhances efficiency and minimizes the risk of overruns. The combination of improved visibility across all resources and engagement financials helps ensure projects remain profitable and on schedule.

AI AND OPTIMIZING TIME, TALENT, AND CAPITAL

AI and Talent Optimization

The resource-based view suggests that a company's unique, valuable, and irreplaceable human capital is a key driver of corporate sustainability and provides a competitive edge (Yildiz & Esmer, 2022). However, there is a need to establish a reliable and effective method for evaluating individual talent potential (Vecchi *et al.*, 2021). Further investigation is required to identify quality, measurable indicators that accurately assess talent potential across various organizational settings. Studies have indicated that a supportive work environment contributes to the development of individual skills. Nevertheless, gaps persist in our understanding of the workplace elements that most significantly impact talent development. Additional research is necessary to identify factors that best facilitate talent growth in the workplace. The application of Artificial Intelligence (AI) to talent management (TM) has emerged as a significant area of study. "Cognitive technologies" and "artificial intelligence" have become ubiquitous terms in business, research, and technology spheres. The incorporation of AI into talent management in higher education institutions marks a notable advancement in both fields. This literature review examined the current research landscape at this intersection, highlighting key findings, gaps, and implications for future studies. Talent management in higher education centers primarily focuses on the recruitment, development, and retention of academic personnel. Amelia and Rofaida (2023) provided a comprehensive overview of talent management practices across various organizations, emphasizing the crucial role of technology in enhancing these practices. Their findings revealed that while technology facilitates improved talent management processes, there is considerable variation in how organizations adopt these technologies. This observation underscores the need for a customized approach in the higher education sector, where institutional requirements and contexts can significantly influence the efficacy of talent management strategies. Similarly, Mattalatta and Andriani (2023) explored the impact of human resource management on organizational performance, highlighting the mediating role of talent management. Their research demonstrated that effective talent management can substantially improve organizational performance, a highly relevant conclusion for education institutions seeking to enhance their academic and administrative effectiveness. These technologies play a crucial role in shaping the interaction between people and technology in business operations (Kuzior & Kwilinski, 2022).

The implementation of cognitive technologies, such as AI, has led to notable technological progress in both commercial and research sectors (Kuzior & Kwilinski, 2022). Contemporary technological solutions address challenges in developing systematic automated information support systems. However, AI has not yet been extensively utilized to enhance employment management practices (Vrontis *et al.*, 2022). Recent studies have explored AI's potential in developing job market interventions (Jarrahi, 2018), though many innovative approaches to improve existing talent management frameworks remain understudied. To modernize workforce management, general-purpose AI technology has been employed to implement changes (Agrawal *et al.*, 2018). The creation of new AI-driven human resource management applications has presented developers with various obstacles, including dehumanization, unjust requirements, and biased algorithms, necessitating thorough investigation (Tambe *et al.*, 2019).

The integration of AI into human resources management is a burgeoning area with far-reaching consequences. A bibliometric study by Palos-Sánchez *et al.* (2022) on AI applications in human resources management revealed that the majority of research concentrated on hiring and selection procedures. This indicates a knowledge gap regarding AI's potential in other HR domains, such as employee development and retention. Their research showed increasing interest in AI applications but emphasized the need for a more comprehensive exploration of AI's capabilities across various HR subfields. Expanding on this, Aboud (2023) examined AI's role in HRM, proposing that AI should be considered a supportive tool rather than a replacement for human judgment. This viewpoint aligns with the broader understanding that AI can augment, not substitute, human abilities. Aboud's (2023) study reinforced the idea that AI can offer significant assistance in talent management by streamlining routine tasks and providing data-driven insights. However, its implementation must be carefully considered to maximize its advantages. The incorporation of AI with talent management strategies in higher education can tackle several challenges identified in existing research. Amelia and Rofaida (2023) underscored the significance of data measurement and analysis in talent management, an area where AI can make substantial contributions through predictive analytics and data-driven insights. AI's capacity to swiftly and accurately analyze large datasets can assist institutions in enhancing their recruitment strategies, identifying skill deficiencies, and customizing development programs to individual requirements.

AI AND TIME OPTIMIZATION

In both professional and personal spheres, the ability to manage time effectively has always been essential. This skill has become even more critical in today's rapidly evolving world. With constant distractions, maintaining focus and productivity can be challenging (Rampton, 2023). The success of an organization depends heavily on efficient time management. In this context, the incorporation of Artificial Intelligence (AI) into tools for tracking and allocating time has emerged as a groundbreaking solution. This article examined how AI-driven precision revolutionizes corporate time management and how innovations, such as planners, are reshaping workplace planning and control.

AI excels in streamlining time-consuming and labor-intensive tasks. It can handle data entry, generate reports, and perform content searches, allowing humans to concentrate on tasks that require cognitive skills. By leveraging AI, companies can reduce the time spent on mundane activities, enabling employees to focus on significant and creative endeavors. AI tools can expedite this process by delivering accurate and relevant results, helping individuals quickly find necessary information. This leads to increased job satisfaction because employees can dedicate their efforts to more meaningful tasks. Additionally, AI enhances decision-making by swiftly analyzing vast amounts of data. It uncovers patterns and trends that are difficult to detect manually, aiding companies in making informed decisions regarding products, marketing strategies, and resource allocation (Rampton, 2023).

AI's data analysis capabilities of AI facilitate the identification of patterns and trends, enabling smarter choices in product development, marketing, and other areas. Utilizing AI, companies can monitor the time spent on various tasks and projects without manually starting or stopping timers. This approach saves time and effort while providing more accurate insights into time usage. AI systems can examine the calendars of multiple individuals to identify potential scheduling conflicts. Proposing alternative times helps avoid overlapping meetings and events. AI can consider factors, such as availability, location, and preferences, to determine optimal meeting times. Consequently, companies can save time and prevent the scheduling of meetings during inconvenient hours.

AI can determine how time is allocated by analyzing a company's calendar. These insights can be used to improve time management, such as scheduling dedicated blocks for specific tasks and avoiding consecutive meetings. AI can automate processes, such as sending meeting reminders, adding new events to calendars, and freeing time for other activities. Ultimately, AI can significantly enhance calendar management and smart scheduling efficiency. By employing AI, companies can save time and resources through task automation, reduction in scheduling conflicts, and improved productivity. AI can also automate the scheduling of tasks, allowing companies to focus on their priorities as time is freed (Amelia & Rofaida, 2023).

AI AND OPTIMIZATION OF CAPITAL

The integration of AI in financial management is revolutionizing corporate practices and decision-making processes. By incorporating sophisticated machine learning algorithms, extensive data analysis, and automated systems, businesses have seen substantial improvements in the precision of financial data, business projections, and investment tactics. AI enables instantaneous examination of vast datasets, revealing patterns and trends that human analysts might overlook, thus enhancing the efficiency of decision-making. Research by Li *et al.* (2023) and Oyeniyi *et al.* (2024) explored the considerable influence of AI on financial management and reporting, emphasizing its impact on areas, such as forecasting, financial analysis, and data-driven decision processes. Furthermore, AI enhances various aspects of financial reporting and analysis by extracting pertinent financial information, refining data, processing information, and alerting finance teams to areas requiring attention. These advancements result in the production of comprehensive financial statements and regulatory reports, ultimately reducing the workload for finance teams. A study by Kanaparthi (2023) illustrated the significant impact of AI and machine learning on accounts payable management. The research addressed issues, such as manual validation procedures, catalogue discrepancies, invoice duplication, and fluctuating tax codes. Moreover, it proposed an AI-powered invoice processing system that significantly reduces manual intervention and associated errors. Additionally, the study suggested an automated risk detection system to identify and prevent duplicate payments and fraudulent transactions. The research indicated that integrating technologies, such as natural language processing for invoice data extraction, machine learning algorithms for anomaly detection, and robotic process automation for repetitive tasks, enhances the efficiency, accuracy, and speed of payables-related transaction processing and execution. In summary, the innovative application of AI in financial management lies in its capacity to automate processes and improve the predictive accuracy of forecasts, as well as the speed and precision of transaction execution and reporting.

In the future, AI systems capable of examining past records, market patterns, and projections of economic indicators will be essential in anticipating upcoming cash flows, shifts in demand, and supply chain issues. This predictive ability will enable companies to generate more precise forecasts and make proactive choices, thus enhancing cash management and minimizing the risk of liquidity problems. Research by Chen *et al.* (2012) reported that AI-powered predictive analytics will boost the precision of financial projections, resulting in improved resource distribution and risk handling. In summary, the upcoming developments in AI for working capital management are poised to bring substantial improvements by incorporating smart systems, facilitating real-time monitoring, and utilizing predictive analytics. These advancements will enhance the accuracy and efficiency of financial processes and strengthen organizations' ability to make strategic decisions. As AI technology progresses, its influence on working capital management will become increasingly significant, leading to improved financial results and promoting sustainable business expansion.

IMPLICATION

The incorporation of AI into resource allocation processes has wide-ranging consequences, presenting both advantages and obstacles for organizations across diverse sectors. A key benefit is the improved capacity for data-informed decision-making. AI's prowess in examining large datasets and producing predictive insights enables companies to maximize their utilization of time, personnel, and finances, resulting in heightened operational efficiency and overall performance.

In the realm of human resources, AI introduces groundbreaking possibilities for hiring, skill development, and employee retention. Firms adopting AI-powered talent management tools can anticipate a more individualized and data-driven approach to staff development, potentially boosting job satisfaction and decreasing turnover rates. This transition may foster more vibrant and competitive work environments where talent is more effectively cultivated and maintained. Regarding financial management, the application of AI in capital allocation impacts both immediate decision-making and long-term strategic planning. AI's capacity to deliver precise financial projections, evaluate risks, and optimize investments offers organizations a considerable edge over competitors. Nevertheless, the growing dependence on AI also raises issues concerning algorithmic bias, data protection, and potential job losses. Organizations must address these challenges and implement AI solutions in a manner that balances innovation with ethical considerations.

To conclude, the integration of AI into resource allocation strategies has the potential to revolutionize industries, offering unprecedented levels of efficiency, effectiveness, and strategic insight. Organizations that successfully navigate the hurdles associated with AI implementation are poised to gain a significant competitive advantage in the global marketplace. The incorporation of AI into resource allocation has far-reaching consequences. Companies that successfully implement AI technologies can gain a competitive edge through enhanced efficiency and better use of resources. Furthermore, the strategic application of AI in optimizing time, human capital, and financial resources can boost organizational flexibility, allowing businesses to respond swiftly to market shifts. Nevertheless, the effective deployment of AI necessitates a cultural transformation within organizations, emphasizing data-centric decision-making and cross-departmental cooperation. Executives must prioritize investments in AI tools and employee training to develop a workforce capable of maximizing AI's benefits in resource allocation.

CONCLUSION

This chapter has delved into the revolutionary impact of Artificial Intelligence (AI) on resource management, particularly in the areas of time, talent, and capital within organizations. AI has proven to be a pivotal force in resource allocation, delivering unprecedented levels of efficiency, accuracy, and strategic insights. By adopting AI technologies, businesses can enhance their operational processes, make informed decisions based on data, and more effectively align their resources with corporate goals. The application of AI in human resource management has demonstrated considerable promise in improving recruitment strategies, recognizing skill deficiencies, and delivering customized employee growth initiatives. Likewise, AI-powered time management tools have shown their worth by automating routine tasks, minimizing idle time, and boosting scheduling effectiveness. Additionally, the incorporation of AI into capital allocation has resulted in more precise financial projections, improved investment choices, and rationalized financial reporting, thereby enhancing overall organizational performance. While AI offers numerous benefits in resource allocation, its implementation also brings challenges, including issues related to data security, algorithmic bias, and the potential dehumanization of certain roles. Nevertheless, as AI technologies continue to advance, these obstacles can be overcome through careful implementation and ongoing innovation. In conclusion, AI's contribution to resource optimization represents a significant advancement in contemporary business practices, equipping organizations with the necessary tools to operate more efficiently in an increasingly competitive landscape.

To sum up, the use of AI-driven resource allocation to optimize time, talent, and capital presents a significant opportunity for organizations aiming to improve their operational efficiency and strategic decision-making processes. As AI technologies advance, their integration into resource management will become increasingly vital. Despite ongoing challenges, the potential advantages of AI in resource allocation are considerable. By adopting these innovations, organizations can position themselves for success in an increasingly competitive environment, ultimately achieving greater sustainability and long-term growth. This research also critically examined the application of Artificial Intelligence in revolutionizing traditional working capital management, a crucial yet often neglected aspect of financial management. It underscored the drawbacks of conventional working capital management methods, such as the prevalence of human errors due to manual intervention, inefficiencies in real-time data analysis and data-driven decision-making, and the lack of a clear understanding of businesses' overall working capital requirements, which expose companies to liquidity and credit risks. Through extensive literature and case study analyses, the research effectively demonstrated how the integration of AI with existing systems achieves optimization and accuracy in forecasting the individual components of working capital, including inventory, accounts receivable, accounts payable, and other current balances on a company's balance sheet.

REFERENCES

Agrawal, A., Gans, J., Goldfarb, A. (2018). Prediction, judgment, and complexity: A theory of decision-making and artificial intelligence. *The Economics of Artificial Intelligence: An Agenda.* University of Chicago Press.

Amelia, E., Rofaida, R. (2023). Talent management in organizations: Systematic literature review. *Airlangga Journal of Innovation Management, 4*(1), 41-59.
[http://dx.doi.org/10.20473/ajim.v4i1.44981]

Asiedu, E., Majeed, M., Charles, A., Fatawu, A. Assessing the influence of self-service technology on wom: The role of customer satisfaction. *Advances in Information Communication Technology and Computing Proceedings of AICTC 2024, 2.*
[http://dx.doi.org/10.1007/978-981-97-6106-7_5]

Charles, A., Arko-Cole, N., Yomboi, J., & Tijani, A. (2023). Emerging use of technologies in education. *Digital Transformation in Education: Emerging Markets and Opportunities, 82–97.*
[http://dx.doi.org/10.2174/9789815124750123010009]

Chen, H., Chiang, R.H.L., Storey, V.C. (2012). Business intelligence and analytics: From big data to big impact. *MIS Quarterly, 36*(4), 1165-1188.
[http://dx.doi.org/10.2307/41703503]

Jarrahi, M.H. (2018). Artificial intelligence and the future of work: Human-AI symbiosis in organizational decision making. *Business Horizons, 61*(4), 577-586.
[http://dx.doi.org/10.1016/j.bushor.2018.03.007]

Kanaparthi, V.K. (2023). Examining the plausible applications of artificial intelligence & machine learning in accounts payable improvement. *FinTech, 2*(3), 461-474.
[http://dx.doi.org/10.3390/fintech2030026]

Khan, F.A., Nawab, A.K., Aamir, A. (2024). Adoption of artificial intelligence in human resource management: An application of TOE-TAM model. *Research and Review: Human Resource and Labour Management, 5*(1), 22-36.

Kuzior, A., Kettler, K., Rąb, Ł. (2022). Great resignation—Ethical, cultural, relational, and personal dimensions of generation Y and Z employees' engagement. *Sustainability (Basel), 14*(11), 6764.
[http://dx.doi.org/10.3390/su14116764]

Li, X., Sigov, A., Ratkin, L., Ivanov, L.A., Li, L. (2023). Artificial intelligence applications in finance: a survey. *Journal of Management Analytics, 10*(4), 676-692.
[http://dx.doi.org/10.1080/23270012.2023.2244503]

Majeed, M., Charles, A., Jonas, Y., Arko-Cole, N., & Tijani, A. (2024). Factors influencing the adoption of online shopping and its influence on consumers' intention to shop online: a study of smes in Ghana. *Digital Transformation in African SMEs: Emerging Issues and Trends,* 30–60.
[http://dx.doi.org/10.2174/9789815223347124020005]

Oyeniyi, D.O., Ugochukwu, C.E., Mhlongo, N.Z. (2024). The influence of AI on financial reporting quality: A critical review and analysis. *World Journal of Advanced Research and Reviews, 22*(1), 679-694.
[http://dx.doi.org/10.30574/wjarr.2024.22.1.1157]

Rampton, J. (2023). The future of AI in time management. LinkedIn. Available from: https://www.linkedin.com/pulse/future-ai-time-management-john-rampton/.

Tambe, P., Cappelli, P., Yakubovich, V. (2019). Artificial intelligence in human resources management: Challenges and a path forward. *California Management Review, 61*(4), 15-42.
[http://dx.doi.org/10.1177/0008125619867910]

Vecchi, A., Della Piana, B., Feola, R., Crudele, C. (2021). Talent management processes and outcomes in a virtual organization. *Business Process Management Journal, 27*(7), 1937-1965.
[http://dx.doi.org/10.1108/BPMJ-06-2019-0227]

Vrontis, D., Christofi, M., Pereira, V., Tarba, S., Makrides, A., Trichina, E. (2022). Artificial intelligence, robotics, advanced technologies and human resource management: a systematic review. *The International Journal of Human Resource Management, 33*(6), 1237-1266.
[http://dx.doi.org/10.1080/09585192.2020.1871398]

Yildiz, R.O., Esmer, S. (2022). Talent management strategies and functions: A systematic review. *Industrial and Commercial Training.*
[http://dx.doi.org/10.1108/ICT-01-2022-0007]

Yomboi, J., Majeed, M., Asiedu, E., Nangpiire, C., Alhassan, F., & Manu, V. (2024). Green blockchain technology for an eco-friendly environment. *Exploring Waste Management in Sustainable Development Contexts,* 219–233.
[http://dx.doi.org/10.4018/979-8-3693-4264-0.ch015]

CHAPTER 7

The Future of Strategic Management: AI and Beyond

Abstract: This chapter explores the implications of Artificial Intelligence (AI) for strategic management, drawing on case studies, empirical research, and industry examples to illustrate the transformative role of AI across various organizational functions. The findings indicate that AI significantly alters strategic management by improving resource allocation, data-driven decision-making, and agile strategic responses. AI enhances efficiency in managing time, capital, and talent while strengthening competitive positioning. Research suggests that AI enables dynamic and adaptive strategic management, making organizations more responsive to market changes. However, concerns regarding the ethical implications, transparency, and potential biases of AI must be addressed to ensure its effective and responsible use in strategy formulation.

Keywords: AI, Adoption, Adaptability, ML, Transformative, Technologies.

INTRODUCTION

As AI transforms global business, strategic management based on competitive advantage and organizational efficiency is changing. Data-driven decision-making, operational optimization, and innovation in complex markets are enabled by AI. Due to machine learning, predictive analytics, and automation, AI is needed for tactical and strategic planning. This chapter entitled "The Future of Strategic Management: AI and Beyond" discusses how AI's evolution is challenging strategic management and the implications, opportunities, and emerging practices reshaping this field. Strategic management has been traditionally focused on resource leveraging, competition response, and value creation through planned objectives and resource allocation. AI helps businesses predict trends, analyze massive data sets, and make complex decisions with unprecedented precision and agility (Kemp, 2024). Businesses predict consumer needs, optimize pricing, and streamline supply chains using real-time data analysis and machine learning algorithms. AI integration switches strategic management from intuition to data, requiring constant learning and adaptation (Rakova *et al.*, 2021). AI-based strategic models may help companies anticipate and respond to market changes faster, giving them an edge.

AI alters operational efficiency and competitive intelligence. Predictive modelling and advanced analytics can accurately assess competitors, market conditions, and consumer sentiment (Benzaid and Taleb, 2020). Organizations gain market share by quickly interpreting and acting on external signals. Strategic agility depends on AI's ability to incorporate new data and learn from trends. Dynamic industries can quickly adapt to consumer preferences and regulatory changes with AI-powered business intelligence systems (Keding, 2021; Asiedu *et al.*, 2024; Charles *et al.*, 2023; Majeed *et al.*, 2024; Yomboi *et al.*, 2024)). AI systems improve productivity, career development, and targeted recruitment, helping companies recruit and retain top talent for strategic goals (Schiff *et al.*, 2020). Predictive analytics helps companies anticipate workforce needs, fill skill gaps, and adapt to AI. Strategic and human capital management are converging to highlight talent as a key competitive advantage.

Nonetheless, AI has drawbacks. Data privacy, accountability, and algorithmic bias complicate strategic AI use. To maintain stakeholder trust, companies must ethically use AI tools, raising transparency and fairness concerns (Vrontis *et al.*, 2023). This book chapter will address these issues and emphasize the need for ethical AI governance frameworks in strategic decision-making. AI improves strategic management decision-making, operational efficiency, and competitiveness. Strategic management traditionally involves making, implementing, and assessing cross-functional decisions to achieve organisational goals (Haleem *et al.*, 2022). Data-driven, predictive, and responsive AI complicates strategic planning and implementation (Henry, 2021). The real-time processing of massive data, pattern recognition, and informed recommendations of AI have changed competitive strategy, resource allocation, and market positioning (Taeihagh, 2021). This chapter examines this rapidly changing landscape and the pros and cons of AI in strategic management.

Marketing trends and customer behavior can be predicted using AI to improve strategic management. Machine learning models can predict future outcomes from historical data, helping organisations adjust strategies (Borges *et al.*, 2021). AI-driven customer data analytics helps marketers personalize outreach and boost customer satisfaction (Libai *et al.*, 2020). This model outperforms historical data and managerial intuition-based strategic management models (Keding, 2021). AI has also transformed the strategic management tool of competitive intelligence. Classic competitive analysis was often slow and static due to manual data collection processes. In contrast, AI allows companies to instantly analyse competitor data, market trends, and industry insights (Vrontis *et al.*, 2023).

Monitoring and responding to the external environment improves an organization's agility, allowing it to respond faster and more accurately to competitive pressures. AI-enabled companies can seize market opportunities and mitigate threats, staying ahead (Sarker, 2022).

AI affects strategic management capital and human resource allocation. Predictive analytics can evaluate talent, identify skill gaps, and optimize recruitment for workforce deployment (Bareis and Katzenbach, 2022). AI algorithms match employee skills regarding projects, increasing productivity and engagement. AI can maximise investment returns, forecast returns, and efficiently allocate capital, improving financial decision-making. AI robo-advisors and financial modeling systems align capital expenditure and investment planning with different strategies (Holmström, 2022). Integrating AI into strategic management raises ethical and operational issues. Organisations must address AI algorithm bias, data privacy, and AI-driven decision-making transparency to build trust and compliance (Lee *et al.*, 2019). Unequal AI governance could harm an organization's reputation and stakeholder trust. AI-driven strategic management requires ethical and transparent policies (Strohm *et al.*, 2020).

This chapter aims to provide a comprehensive exploration of the implications of AI for strategic management, drawing upon case studies, empirical research, and industry examples to illustrate the role of AI across various functions within organizations. Additionally, it addresses emerging trends and future directions for AI in strategic management, including the anticipated influence of quantum computing, reinforcement learning, and autonomous decision-making systems on the strategic capabilities of firms. By examining both the benefits and limitations of AI, this chapter will provide readers with insights into how they can strategically navigate the rapidly advancing landscape of AI and leverage it to foster innovation, efficiency, and competitive positioning in their own organizations.

Historical Background of AI in Strategic Management

In recent decades, advancements in computing and data science have enabled the integration of AI into strategic management. In the 1950s and 1960s, computational power supported basic decision models, laying the groundwork for AI in business strategies (Henry, 2021). These early applications focused on operation research and optimization with limited data processing and prediction. Technological advancements and theoretical developments have laid the groundwork for the gradual integration of AI into strategic management (Maedche *et al.*, 2019).

In the 1980s, expert systems changed the strategic management of AI. These systems were among the first to mimic domain expertise and simulate human decision-making. Finance, healthcare, and manufacturing companies used expert systems to interpret structured data and make rule-based strategic planning recommendations (Borges *et al.*, 2021). Expert systems captured and applied specialized knowledge to help organizations make strategic decisions in complex, data-intensive environments. Despite their rigid programming and lack of adaptability, expert systems showed that AI could support strategic decisions, especially in situations requiring rapid, knowledge-driven responses (Libai *et al.*, 2020).

In the late 1990s and early 2000s, Data-driven Decision Support Systems (DSS) made strategic applications more flexible and robust. DSS improved data processing and visualization to analyze market trends, forecast outcomes, and improve strategic decisions using structured and unstructured data (Zhang and Lu, 2021). Unlike rule-based systems, DSS could process large amounts of data and provide real-time strategic insights and competitive landscapes. Data were emphasised in strategic planning, setting the stage for the big data revolution that would transform the role of AI in management (Vrontis *et al.*, 2023). In 2010, machine learning and big data analytics improved AI strategic management. Unlike earlier systems, machine learning models can analyze massive amounts of unstructured data, learn from patterns, and make predictions without programming. Real-time data processing and machine learning algorithms enable dynamic forecasting, trend analysis, and customer insights, improving AI's strategic role (Brynjolfsson *et al.*, 2019). AI-driven analytics have helped Google and Amazon compete by focusing on personalization, predictive modeling, and operational efficiency (Xu *et al.*, 2019).

After a rapid transition from static, rule-based systems to sophisticated machine learning applications, AI now dominates strategic management through predictive analytics, optimization algorithms, and autonomous decision-making systems. AI optimises resources and adapts strategies in real time for supply chain and customer relationship management.

AI-driven strategic management replaces periodic strategic planning with an adaptive model that uses data to inform and refine strategic decisions (Panda *et al.*, 2019). AI's predictive and prescriptive capabilities provide organisations with new insights into long-term planning and competitive positioning (Enholm *et al.*, 2022). AI in strategic management has progressed from early decision support systems to data-driven models capable of handling complex, adaptive tasks. AI may enhance strategic management by automating decision-making and integrating business functions. This historical perspective shows how AI has advanced strategic management, demonstrating its potential to innovate and transform competitive strategies across industries. Fig. (**1**) below provides a detailed visual representation of the study's findings.

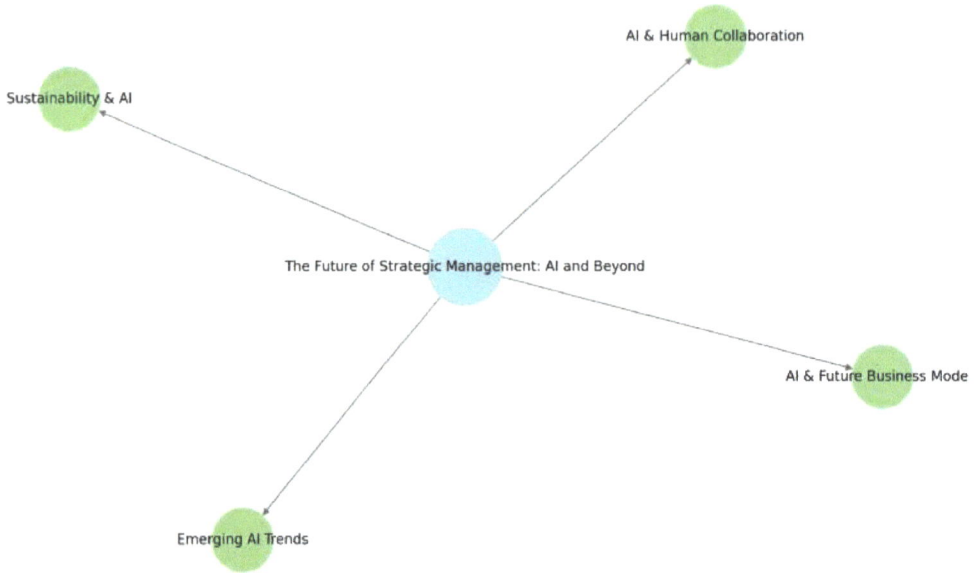

Fig. (1). Conceptual framework.

CORE AI TECHNOLOGIES AND THEIR APPLICATIONS IN STRATEGIC MANAGEMENT

Core AI technologies improve strategic decision-making, forecasting, and operational efficiency, boosting strategic management. Companies using data and automated insights to gain a competitive edge need machine learning, NLP, computer vision, and robotics (Haleem *et al.*, 2022). In today's fast-paced, information-intensive environment, AI technologies help businesses analyze complex data sets, automate routine processes, and make data-driven decisions for strategic management.

Machine Learning

Machine Learning (ML) has transformed strategic management by identifying patterns, predicting outcomes, and improving decision-making models with new data. Learning from data without programming, ML algorithms improve customer segmentation, demand forecasting, and risk management (Henry, 2021). Machine learning algorithms help Amazon and Walmart make timely, data-driven decisions that improve customer satisfaction and operational efficiency by analyzing historical purchasing data to predict future trends and optimise inventory management (Kemp, 2024). ML can assess credit risk, detect fraud, and optimise financal portfolios, demonstrating its flexibility and power in strategic management across different sectors (Borges *et al.*, 2021).

Natural Language Processing (NLP)

Natural Language Processing helps AI systems understand, interpret, and generate human language for strategic management. NLP excels at strategic planning with unstructured social media, customer reviews, and internal communication data. NLP tools help companies understand customer preferences, market sentiment, and brand perception by analysing and identifying trends in massive text data (Sjödin *et al.*, 2021). Airbnb and Netflix use NLP to analyze user feedback and adapt to changing customer needs in real-time (Vrontis *et al.*, 2023). NLP-driven chatbots and virtual assistants streamline customer service, reduce costs, improve customer experience, and align with organizational strategies.

Computer Vision

Strategic management sectors that analyze images and videos can benefit from computer vision, which lets AI systems interpret and process visual data. Computer vision lets machines "see" and understand visual data for quality control, security, and customer interaction. Computer vision technology detects manufacturing defects and monitors product quality, helping companies meet standards and reduce waste (Tschang and Almirall, 2021). Computer vision enhances retail customer convenience and engagement with virtual try-ons and autonomous checkouts (Allen, 2019). It also boosts operational efficiency, customer satisfaction, and innovation in these applications.

Robotic Process Automation (RPA)

RPA automates rule-based tasks so workers can focus on strategy. RPA bots speed up and improve data entry, transaction processing, and report generation, boosting productivity and lowering costs. In sectors like banking and insurance, RPA automates back-office processes, freeing up resources for strategic analysis and customer engagement (Sarker, 2022). Companies like Deloitte and IBM use RPA to automate finance, HR, and IT tasks, enhancing agility and supporting strategic goals (Enholm *et al.*, 2022). Additionally, its scalability enables companies to respond quickly to market demands.

Predictive and Prescriptive Analytics

Advanced machine learning models predict and optimize business outcomes with predictive and prescriptive analytics. Predicting future trends using historical data helps companies plan strategically. By optimizing outcomes, prescriptive analytics guides strategic decision-making (Lee *et al.*, 2019). Predictive models help Coca-Cola forecast demand, optimize stock, and avoid costly supply chain disruptions (Criado and Gil-Garcia, 2019). Prescriptive analytics helps marketers identify customer preferences and recommend engagement strategies for revenue growth and retention. Machine learning, NLP, computer vision, RPA, and predictive analytics improve strategic management. All these technologies automate, analyze, or inform decisions. These AI technologies will make strategic management more agile and data-driven, optimizing resource allocation and competitive positioning in complex environments.

IMPACT OF AI ON KEY STRATEGIC MANAGEMENT AREAS

The integration of Artificial Intelligence (AI) into strategic management has revolutionized the way organizations operate, fundamentally altering key areas, such as decision-making, resource allocation, market analysis, and competitive advantage. This transformation is driven by the capabilities of AI to analyze vast datasets, recognize patterns, and generate insights that were previously unattainable through traditional methods

Enhancing Decision-making Processes

Data analytics and machine learning improve organizational decision-making. AI algorithms can spot trends and predict outcomes, helping businesses make better strategic decisions. AI-driven predictive analytics aids market demand planning (Haleem *et al.*, 2022). AI-based decision-making facilitates market adaptation by improving accuracy and speed (Henry, 2021). AI processes large amounts of data quickly to make real-time decisions. This significantly aids fast-paced industries that require quick decisions. AI systems can analyze market data and execute trades in milliseconds, seizing financial opportunities humans might miss (Zuiderwijk *et al.*, 2021). The shift toward data-driven decision-making shows the strategic value of AI in organizational management.

Optimizing Resource Allocation

AI optimises the resource allocation function within strategic management. Historical data and subjective judgment are inefficient resource allocation methods. However, AI algorithms can optimise time, talent, and capital allocation using multiple data sources (Borges *et al.*, 2021). AI-powered tools can assess employee performance and skills, helping companies prioritise projects (Libai *et al.*, 2020). Further, AI has altered capital allocation strategies in financial management. Machine learning models can predict ROI and advise investment decisions related to both CapEx and OpEx (Wirtz *et al.*, 2019). Ultimately, data - driven resource allocation boosts efficiency and strategic goals.

Transforming Market Analysis and Competitive Intelligence

AI has transformed market analysis and competitive intelligence by uncovering consumer behavior and emerging trends. It can analyze data from social media, customers, and markets to inform strategic marketing and product development (Coombs *et al.*, 2020). AI algorithms support demographic-targeted marketing by effectively segmenting customers. Additionally, AI continuously monitors markets and competitors, enhancing competitive intelligence. With advanced AI systems, companies can rapidly respond to competitors' pricing strategies, marketing efforts, and product launches (Vrontis *et al.*, 2023). In today's fast-changing business environment, such agility in market positioning is essential.

Driving Innovation and Strategic Agility

AI helps companies create customer-focused goods and services, and AI-driven R&D meets market needs (Sarker, 2022). Company innovation risks are reduced by AI models that simulate market scenarios and test strategies before implementation. AI also helps companies react quickly to market disruptions and accelerates their adaptation to new opportunities (Enholm *et al.*, 2022). As technology and consumer preferences evolve, adaptability becomes key. AI has deep and complex effects on strategic management. It improves decision-making, resource allocation, market analysis, and innovation, helping companies adapt to changing business conditions. AI is likely to become increasingly integrated into strategic management, creating new opportunities and challenges for global organizations.

Challenges and Ethical Considerations in AI-Driven Strategic Management

Although AI in strategic management offers many benefits, it also raises ethical concerns. As companies increasingly rely on AI for strategic decision-making, various issues can impact both its effectiveness and public acceptability. Organizations using AI in this context face ethical, data-related, and cultural challenges.

In AI-driven strategic management, AI ethics are complex. AI system deployment raises fairness, accountability, and transparency concerns. Training data biases may cause AI algorithms to discriminate (Bani Ahmad, 2024). Unfair recruitment, performance evaluations, and customer interactions undermine system fairness. Organisations need ethical frameworks to prevent bias and regulate AI use (Aldoseri *et al.*, 2023). The lack of AI decision-making transparency raises another ethical concern. Many AI algorithms, especially deep learning ones, are "black boxes," making stakeholder decisions uncertain (Lauterbach, 2019). This opacity can make customers, investors, and employees doubt the company's ethics. Therefore, organizations must prioritize explainability in AI systems to ensure transparent and accountable decision-making (Nassar and Kamal, 2021).

Quality training and decision-making data determine the success of AI in strategic management. Poor data quality can reduce AI's value by causing inaccurate predictions and decisions. Companies need strong data governance frameworks to ensure the integrity, accuracy, and relevance of AI system data (Walz and Firth-Butterfield, 2019). Regular data audits, validation, and understanding of data sources are necessary. Privacy and data quality are among the biggest challenges in AI-driven strategic management. Organizations often find GDPR and CCPA data privacy regulations complex. Compliance with these regulations is essential to avoid legal issues and safeguard sensitive data (Yaseen, 2023). Additionally, organizations must enforce data privacy policies to avoid financial and reputational harm.

Organizational culture and readiness for change affect the implementation of AI in strategic management. Many workers worry that AI will negatively impact their jobs and workflows. Anti-AI sentiment can slow adoption and reduce potential benefits (Keding, 2021). To overcome these barriers, organizations should emphasize innovation, collaboration, and AI's role in enhancing human capabilities. AI-driven strategic management may require significant organizational and process changes. Reorganising hierarchies may help teams use AI for agile decision-making and cross-functional collaboration (Schiff *et al.*, 2020). Furthermore, employers must train workers to use AI systems and embrace AI-driven strategic management.

AI in strategic management improves decision-making, resource optimization, and innovation, but it also raises ethical concerns. To implement AI effectively, organizations must address issues of bias, fairness, data quality, privacy, and cultural resistance. Addressing these issues can help organizations maximize the potential of AI while maintaining ethical standards and stakeholder trust.

FUTURE TRENDS AND DIRECTIONS IN AI-DRIVEN STRATEGIC MANAGEMENT

Emerging Technologies Impacting Strategic Management

New technologies that enhance AI capabilities are a major trend in AI-driven strategic management. Reinforcement learning enables AI systems to make complex decisions by learning from their environment. Companies can use this technology to simulate resource allocation and risk management strategies (Kemp, 2024). Quantum computing has the potential to transform AI by significantly accelerating complex computational processes. This advancement may improve predictive analytics, scenario modeling, and strategic forecasting, enabling companies to make more informed decisions (Sestino and De-Mauro, 2022). AI-enabled IoT devices are also expected to enhance data collection and analysis. AI algorithms can optimize operations and strategic decision-making by leveraging vast amounts of real-time IoT data (Benzaid and Taleb, 2020). As IoT increasingly connects organizations, effective data management will become essential for maintaining competitiveness.

The Evolving Role of AI in Strategic Resource Allocation

Resource allocation will become more complex as AI continues to advance. AI will assist companies in allocating resources and analyzing complex datasets. AI algorithms can identify resource usage patterns to help organizations more effectively allocate capital, talent, and time (Keding, 2021). This data-driven approach to resource allocation may enhance operational efficiency and support strategic initiatives. Companies can allocate resources proactively by using AI-powered predictive analytics to predict market trends and customer behavior. The ability to analyze historical data and forecast future outcomes enables more informed decisions regarding products, marketing strategies, and investments (Koroteev and Tekic, 2021). This proactive resource allocation will help companies adapt to market changes and seize new opportunities.

Integration of Ethical Considerations in AI Strategy

Ethics in AI strategies will become increasingly important as organizations adopt AI-driven strategic management. Customers, employees, and regulators are growing more concerned about AI ethics. Therefore, organisations need strong ethical frameworks to guide AI initiatives and ensure transparency, accountability, and fairness in decision-making (Eboigbe *et al.*, 2023). Explainable AI (XAI) will gain prominence as companies seek to build trust in their AI systems. Explainable AI explains how AI algorithms make decisions, helping stakeholders understand and accept them (Favour Oluwadamilare Usman *et al.*, 2024). Hence, companies must invest in ethical and transparent AI solutions.

Collaborative AI Systems and Human-AI Partnerships

The future of AI-driven strategic management will involve collaborative AI systems working alongside human decision-makers. AI will enhance human judgment, enabling better decision-making (Giuggioli and Pellegrini, 2023). The collaboration between AI and human intuition in addressing complex strategic problems is expected to drive innovation. Additionally, companies must train their employees in AI tools and methodologies to effectively integrate AI into decision-making processes (Allioui and Mourdi, 2023). As AI roles, ethics, and emerging technologies evolve, organizations must adapt quickly and leverage AI to improve decision-making, resource allocation, and operational efficiency. Embracing these changes and fostering human-AI collaboration will help companies maintain a competitive edge.

Case Studies and Industry Applications

Implementing AI and AI-driven solutions in strategic management is transforming industries. Industry case studies show how AI has improved healthcare, finance, manufacturing, and retail operations, decision-making, and competitiveness. Industry case studies highlight AI applications in predictive analytics, automation, personalization, and risk management. This review presents insights from successful AI-integrated companies, sharing their best practices and challenges encountered during implementation.

AI in Healthcare

AI has advanced healthcare by improving diagnosis, patient management, and resource allocation. Drug discovery, predictive analytics, diagnostic imaging, and personalized treatment plans all utilize AI. IBM Watson and Mayo Clinic use AI to identify patient data patterns, improve diagnostic accuracy, and enable precision medicine (Rong *et al.*, 2020). Clinicians can intervene earlier and reduce complications by using Google's DeepMind AI models to predict acute kidney injury up to 48 hours in advance (Arif *et al.*, 2024). These cases demonstrate how AI improves patient outcomes, healthcare efficiency, and hospital operations. However, the benefits of artificial intelligenceare difficult to weigh against ethical and privacy concerns, especially regarding patient data.

AI in Finance

AI has transformed financial risk assessment, fraud detection, investment management, and customer service. AI algorithms help banks make data-driven investment decisions and personalize client recommendations. JPMorgan Chase uses AI-driven predictive analytics to analyze market trends and optimize trading strategies, enabling faster and more informed decisions (Veile *et al.*, 2020). Betterment and Wealthfront's AI-managed, risk-based portfolios make investing more affordable (Rogerson and Parry, 2020). AI-powered Mastercard fraud detection systems analyze transaction patterns in real-time, reducing losses and enhancing security (Aabid *et al.*, 2021). These applications demonstrate how AI can improve financial operational efficiency and customer trust despite challenges related to algorithmic transparency and data bias.

AI in Manufacturing

AI has improved manufacturing through predictive maintenance, quality control, and supply chain optimization. AI and IoT monitor machine performance and predict maintenance needs on GE's Predix platform, reducing downtime and optimising operational efficiency (Bhatt *et al.*, 2019). Siemens uses AI to detect defects in real-time through visual data analysis, enhancing product quality and reducing waste (Dolgui *et al.*, 2019). Machine learning algorithms optimize Amazon's inventory management and delivery routes, lowering operational costs and increasing customer satisfaction (Jandyal *et al.*, 2022). These examples demonstrate how AI enhances manufacturing efficiency, quality, and market agility.

AI in Retail

Personalization, demand forecasting, and dynamic pricing of AI have transformed retail. Walmart and Target use AI to forecast demand and manage inventory, ensuring products are available when customers need them (Neves *et al.*, 2020). Amazon's AI-powered product recommendations, based on browsing history and preferences, have increased sales and customer engagement (Vafadar *et al.*, 2021). Personalization and AI-powered chatbots are now standard customer service tools, improving shopping experiences through immediate assistance. These applications demonstrate how AI can help retailers understand customer behavior, predict market trends, and streamline operations, but data privacy and algorithmic transparency are crucial.

Success Factors and Lessons Learned

The case studies demonstrate several success factors for AI implementation across sectors. A good data infrastructure is essential for AI applications. Companies must optimize data collection, storage, and processing to support AI-driven solutions (Vafadar *et al.*, 2021).

Technical teams and business strategists must collaborate to align AI initiatives with strategic goals and use AI insights in decision-making (Almutairi *et al.*, 2021). Executive commitment to AI-ready culture affects AI adoption and sustainability. Our case studies demonstrate how AI can transform industries while emphasizing ethics and adaptation. Thus, organizations can leverage AI in strategic management by learning from the successes and failures of early adopters.

CONCLUSION

Strategic management research shows that AI transforms organizational strategy in many ways. Through machine learning, predictive analytics, and automation, AI enhances resource allocation, data-driven decision-making, and agile strategic responses. It optimizes the use of time, capital, and talent while strengthening competitive positioning, enabling dynamic and adaptive strategic management. However, alongside these opportunities, AI raises concerns related to data quality, bias, transparency, and ethical governance. While AI has the potential to revolutionize this field, its associated risks must be carefully managed.

Implications for Practitioners and Scholars

Researchers advise practitioners to carefully integrate AI into strategic frameworks. If organizations address the associated challenges, AI can improve decision-making, resource use, and market responsiveness. To maximize AI's potential, practitioners should prioritize ethical frameworks, transparency in AI processes, and a collaborative AI-ready culture. The literature advises investing heavily in talent, skill development, and infrastructure for AI. In addition, the effects of AI should be studied across industries, especially underexplored ones and SMEs. Further research into ethical, environmental, and cross-functional AI adoption may explain AI-driven strategic management.

AI will transform strategic management goal-setting and achievement, potentially integrating into all aspects of business, from efficiency to competitive strategy. Quantum computing will boost AI, so organizations must remain flexible, ethical, and committed to continuous learning. Organizations must carefully implement AI to improve human decision-making, not replace it. Lastly, responsible and sustainable AI-driven strategic management requires research, adaptability, and ethics.

REFERENCES

Aabid, A., Raheman, M.A., Ibrahim, Y.E., Anjum, A., Hrairi, M., Parveez, B., Parveen, N., Mohammed Zayan, J. (2021). A systematic review of piezoelectric materials and energy harvesters for industrial applications. *Sensors, 21*(12)
[http://dx.doi.org/10.3390/s21124145]

Aldoseri, A., Al-Khalifa, K.N., Hamouda, A.M. (2023). Re-Thinking Data Strategy and Integration for Artificial Intelligence: Concepts, Opportunities, and Challenges. *Applied Sciences (Switzerland), 13*(12)
[http://dx.doi.org/10.3390/app13127082]

Allen, G. C. (2019). Understanding China's AI Strategy: Clues to Chinese Strategic Thinking on Artificial Intelligence and National Security. In Center for a New American Security (Issue February, pp. 1–22). globalhha.com. Available from:https://www.cnas.org/publications/reports/understanding-chinas-ai-strategy.

Allioui, H., Mourdi, Y. (2023). Unleashing the Potential of AI: Investigating Cutting-Edge Technologies That Are Transforming Businesses. *International Journal of Computer Engineering and Data Science, 3*(2),

2737-8543. Available from:https://ijceds.com/ijceds/article/view/59/25

Almutairi, A.L., Tayeh, B.A., Adesina, A., Isleem, H.F., Zeyad, A.M. (2021). Potential applications of geopolymer concrete in construction: A review. *Case Studies in Construction Materials.* Elsevier. [http://dx.doi.org/10.1016/j.cscm.2021.e00733]

Arif, H., Kumar, A., Fahad, M., Hussain, H.K. (2024). Future Horizons: AI-Enhanced Threat Detection in Cloud Environments: Unveiling Opportunities for Research. *International Journal of Multidisciplinary Sciences and Arts, 2*(2), 242-251. [http://dx.doi.org/10.47709/ijmdsa.v2i2.3452]

Asiedu, E., Majeed, M., Charles, A., Fatawu, A. (2024). Assessing the Influence of Self-service Technology on WOM: The Role of Customer Satisfaction. *Conference on Advances.* [http://dx.doi.org/10.1007/978-981-97-6106-7_5]

Ahmad, A.Y.A.B. (2024). Ethical implications of artificial intelligence in accounting: A framework for responsible ai adoption in multinational corporations in Jordan. *International Journal of Data and Network Science, 8*(1), 401-414. [http://dx.doi.org/10.5267/j.ijdns.2023.9.014]

Bareis, J., Katzenbach, C. (2022). Talking AI into Being: The Narratives and Imaginaries of National AI Strategies and Their Performative Politics. *Science Technology and Human Values, 47*(5), 855-881. [http://dx.doi.org/10.1177/01622439211030007]

Benzaid, C., Taleb, T. (2020). AI-Driven Zero Touch Network and Service Management in 5G and Beyond: Challenges and Research Directions. *IEEE Network, 34*(2), 186-194. [http://dx.doi.org/10.1109/MNET.001.1900252]

Bhatt, A., Priyadarshini, S., Acharath Mohanakrishnan, A., Abri, A., Sattler, M., Techapaphawit, S. (2019). Physical, chemical, and geotechnical properties of coal fly ash: A global review. *Case Studies in Construction Materials.* Elsevier. [http://dx.doi.org/10.1016/j.cscm.2019.e00263]

Borges, A.F.S., Laurindo, F.J.B., Spínola, M.M., Gonçalves, R.F., Mattos, C.A. (2021). The strategic use of artificial intelligence in the digital era: Systematic literature review and future research directions. *International Journal of Information Management, 57*, 102225. [http://dx.doi.org/10.1016/j.ijinfomgt.2020.102225]

Brynjolfsson, E., Rock, D., & Syverson, C. (2019). Artificial Intelligence and the Modern Productivity Paradox. *The Economics of Artificial Intelligence* 23–60. [http://dx.doi.org/10.7208/chicago/9780226613475.003.0001]

Charles, A., Arko-Cole, N., Yomboi, J., & Tijani, A. (2023). Emerging Use of Technologies in Education. *Digital Transformation in Education: Emerging Markets and Opportunities*, 82–97. [http://dx.doi.org/10.2174/9789815124750123010009]

Coombs, C., Hislop, D., Taneva, S. K., & Barnard, S. (2020). The strategic impacts of Intelligent Automation for knowledge and service work: An interdisciplinary review. In Journal of Strategic Information Systems (Vol. 29, Issue 4). Elsevier. [http://dx.doi.org/10.1016/j.jsis.2020.101600]

Criado, J. I., & Gil-Garcia, J. R. (2019). Creating public value through smart technologies and strategies: From digital services to artificial intelligence and beyond. In International Journal of Public Sector Management (Vol. 32, Issue 5, pp. 438–450). emerald.com. . [http://dx.doi.org/10.1108/IJPSM-07-2019-0178]

Dolgui, A., Ivanov, D., Sethi, S.P., Sokolov, B. (2019). Scheduling in production, supply chain and Industry 4.0 systems by optimal control: fundamentals, state-of-the-art and applications. *International Journal of Production Research, 57*(2), 411-432. [http://dx.doi.org/10.1080/00207543.2018.1442948]

Enholm, I. M., Papagiannidis, E., Mikalef, P., & Krogstie, J. (2022). Artificial Intelligence and Business

Value: a Literature Review. In Information Systems Frontiers (Vol. 24, Issue 5, pp. 1709–1734). Springer. [http://dx.doi.org/10.1007/s10796-021-10186-w]

Giuggioli, G., & Pellegrini, M. M. (2023). Artificial intelligence as an enabler for entrepreneurs: a systematic literature review and an agenda for future research. In International Journal of Entrepreneurial Behaviour and Research (Vol. 29, Issue 4, pp. 816–837). emerald.com. [http://dx.doi.org/10.1108/IJEBR-05-2021-0426]

Haleem, A., Javaid, M., Qadri, M.A., Singh, R.P. (2022). Artificial intelligence (AI) applications for marketing: A literature-based study. *International Journal of.*Elsevier. Available from:https://www.sciencedirect.com/science/article/pii/S2666603022000136 [http://dx.doi.org/10.1016/j.ijin.2022.08.005]

Henry, A. E. (2021). Understanding Strategic Management. In Understanding Strategic Management. Available from:books.google.com. [http://dx.doi.org/10.1093/hebz/9780198859833.001.0001]

Holmström, J. (2022). From AI to digital transformation: The AI readiness framework. In Business Horizons (Vol. 65, Issue 3, pp. 329–339). Elsevier. [http://dx.doi.org/10.1016/j.bushor.2021.03.006]

Jandyal, A., Chaturvedi, I., Wazir, I., Raina, A., Ul Haq, M.I. (2022). 3D printing – A review of processes, materials and applications in industry 4.0. *Sustainable Operations and Computers.* Elsevier. [http://dx.doi.org/10.1016/j.susoc.2021.09.004]

Keding, C. (2021). Understanding the interplay of artificial intelligence and strategic management: four decades of research in review. *Management Review Quarterly, 71*(1), 91-134. [http://dx.doi.org/10.1007/s11301-020-00181-x]

Kemp, A. (2024). Competitive Advantage Through Artificial Intelligence: Toward a Theory of Situated AI. *Academy of Management Review, 49*(3), 618-635. [http://dx.doi.org/10.5465/amr.2020.0205]

Koroteev, D., Tekic, Z. (2021). Artificial intelligence in oil and gas upstream: Trends, challenges, and scenarios for the future. *Energy and AI.* Elsevier. [http://dx.doi.org/10.1016/j.egyai.2020.100041]

Lauterbach, A. (2019). Artificial intelligence and policy: quo vadis? *Digital Policy, Regulation and Governance, 21*(3), 238-263. [http://dx.doi.org/10.1108/DPRG-09-2018-0054]

Lee, J., Suh, T., Roy, D., & Baucus, M. (2019). Emerging technology and business model innovation: The case of artificial intelligence. In Journal of Open Innovation: Technology, Market, and Complexity (Vol. 5, Issue 3). Elsevier. [http://dx.doi.org/10.3390/joitmc5030044]

Libai, B., Bart, Y., Gensler, S., Hofacker, C.F., Kaplan, A., Kötterheinrich, K., Kroll, E.B. (2020). Brave New World? On AI and the Management of Customer Relationships. *Journal of Interactive Marketing, 51*(1), 44-56. [http://dx.doi.org/10.1016/j.intmar.2020.04.002]

Majeed, M., Charles, A., Jonas, Y., Arko-Cole, N., & Tijani, A. (2024). Factors Influencing the Adoption of Online Shopping and Its Influence on Consumers' Intention to Shop Online: A Study of SMEs in Ghana. Digital Transformation in African SMEs: Emerging Issues and Trends, 30–60. [http://dx.doi.org/10.2174/9789815223347124020005]

Maedche, A., Legner, C., Benlian, A., Berger, B., Gimpel, H., Hess, T., Hinz, O., Morana, S., Söllner, M. (2019). AI-Based Digital Assistants. *Business and Information Systems Engineering, 61*(4), 535-544. [http://dx.doi.org/10.1007/s12599-019-00600-8]

Nassar, A., Kamal, M. (2021). Ethical Dilemmas in AI-Powered Decision-Making: A Deep Dive into Big Data-Driven Ethical Considerations. *International Journal of Responsible Artificial Intelligence, 11*(8), 1-11.

Available from:https://neuralslate.com/index.php/Journal-of-Responsible-AI/article/view/43

Neves, A., Godina, R., Azevedo, S.G., Matias, J.C.O. (2020). A comprehensive review of industrial symbiosis. *Journal of Cleaner Production, 247*, 119113.
[http://dx.doi.org/10.1016/j.jclepro.2019.119113]

Panda, G., Upadhyay, A.K., Khandelwal, K. (2019). Artificial Intelligence: A Strategic Disruption in Public Relations. *Journal of Creative Communications, 14*(3), 196-213.
[http://dx.doi.org/10.1177/0973258619866585]

Rakova, B., Yang, J., Cramer, H., Chowdhury, R. (2021). Where Responsible AI meets Reality: Practitioner Perspectives on Enablers for Shifting Organizational Practices. *Proceedings of the ACM on Human-Computer Interaction, 5.*
[http://dx.doi.org/10.1145/3449081]

Rogerson, M., Parry, G.C. (2020). Blockchain: case studies in food supply chain visibility. *Supply Chain Management, 25*(5), 601-614.
[http://dx.doi.org/10.1108/SCM-08-2019-0300]

Rong, G., Mendez, A., Bou Assi, E., Zhao, B., & Sawan, M. (2020). Artificial Intelligence in Healthcare: Review and Prediction Case Studies. In Engineering (Vol. 6, Issue 3, pp. 291–301). Elsevier.
[http://dx.doi.org/10.1016/j.eng.2019.08.015]

Sarker, I. H. (2022). AI-Based Modeling: Techniques, Applications and Research Issues Towards Automation, Intelligent and Smart Systems. In SN Computer Science (Vol. 3, Issue 2). Springer.
[http://dx.doi.org/10.1007/s42979-022-01043-x]

Schiff, D., Biddle, J., Borenstein, J., & Laas, K. (2020). What's next for AI ethics, policy, and governance? A global overview. AIES 2020 - Proceedings of the AAAI/ACM Conference on AI, Ethics, and Society, 153–158.
[http://dx.doi.org/10.1145/3375627.3375804]

Sestino, A., De Mauro, A. (2022). Leveraging Artificial Intelligence in Business: Implications, Applications and Methods. *Technology Analysis and Strategic Management, 34*(1), 16-29.
[http://dx.doi.org/10.1080/09537325.2021.1883583]

Sjödin, D., Parida, V., Palmié, M., Wincent, J. (2021). How AI capabilities enable business model innovation: Scaling AI through co-evolutionary processes and feedback loops. *Journal of Business Research.* Elsevier.
[http://dx.doi.org/10.1016/j.jbusres.2021.05.009]

Strohm, L., Hehakaya, C., Ranschaert, E. R., Boon, W. P. C., & Moors, E. H. M. (2020). Implementation of artificial intelligence (AI) applications in radiology: hindering and facilitating factors. In European Radiology (Vol. 30, Issue 10, pp. 5525–5532). Springer.
[http://dx.doi.org/10.1007/s00330-020-06946-y]

Taeihagh, A. (2021). Governance of artificial intelligence. *Policy and Society, 40*(2), 137-157.
[http://dx.doi.org/10.1080/14494035.2021.1928377]

Tschang, F.T., Almirall, E. (2021). Artificial intelligence as augmenting automation: Implications for employment. *Academy of Management Perspectives, 35*(4), 642-659.
[http://dx.doi.org/10.5465/amp.2019.0062]

Vafadar, A., Guzzomi, F., Rassau, A., & Hayward, K. (2021). Advances in metal additive manufacturing: A review of common processes, industrial applications, and current challenges. In Applied Sciences (Switzerland) (Vol. 11, Issue 3, pp. 1–33).
[http://dx.doi.org/10.3390/app11031213]

Veile, J. W., Kiel, D., Müller, J. M., & Voigt, K. I. (2020). Lessons learned from Industry 4.0 implementation in the German manufacturing industry. In Journal of Manufacturing Technology Management (Vol. 31, Issue 5, pp. 977–997). emerald.com.
[http://dx.doi.org/10.1108/JMTM-08-2018-0270]

Vrontis, D., Christofi, M., Pereira, V., Tarba, S., Makrides, A., & Trichina, E. (2023). Artificial intelligence, robotics, advanced technologies and human resource management: a systematic review. Artificial Intelligence and International HRM, 172–201.
[http://dx.doi.org/10.4324/9781003377085-7]

Walz, A., & Firth-Butterfield, K. (2019). Implementing ethics into artificial intelligence: a contribution, from legal perspective, to the development of an AI governance regime. Duke Law and Technology Review, 18(1), 176. Available from:https://heinonline.org/hol-cgi-bin/get_pdf.cgi?handle=hein.journals/dltr18&section=17.

Wirtz, B.W., Weyerer, J.C., Geyer, C. (2019). Artificial Intelligence and the Public Sector—Applications and Challenges. *International Journal of Public Administration, 42*(7), 596-615.
[http://dx.doi.org/10.1080/01900692.2018.1498103]

Xu, F., Uszkoreit, H., Du, Y., Fan, W., Zhao, D., & Zhu, J. (2019). Explainable AI: A Brief Survey on History, Research Areas, Approaches and Challenges. Lecture Notes in Computer Science (Including Subseries Lecture Notes in Artificial Intelligence and Lecture Notes in Bioinformatics), 11839 LNAI, 563–574.
[http://dx.doi.org/10.1007/978-3-030-32236-6_51]

Yaseen, A. (2023). Ai-Driven Threat Detection and Response: a Paradigm Shift in Cybersecurity. *International Journal of Information and Cybersecurity, 7*(12), 25-43. Available from:https://publications.dlpress.org/index.php/ijic/article/view/73

Yomboi, J., Majeed, M., Asiedu, E., Nangpiire, C., Alhassan, F., & Manu, V. (2024). Green blockchain technology for an eco-friendly environment. Exploring Waste Management in Sustainable Development Contexts, 219–233.
[http://dx.doi.org/10.4018/979-8-3693-4264-0.ch015]

Zhang, C., Lu, Y. (2021). Study on artificial intelligence: The state of the art and future prospects. *Journal of Industrial Information Integration, 23*, 100224.
[http://dx.doi.org/10.1016/j.jii.2021.100224]

Zuiderwijk, A., Chen, Y. C., & Salem, F. (2021). Implications of the use of artificial intelligence in public governance: A systematic literature review and a research agenda. In Government Information Quarterly (Vol. 38, Issue 3). Elsevier.
[http://dx.doi.org/10.1016/j.giq.2021.101577]

SUBJECT INDEX

W

www.ingramcontent.com/pod-product-compliance
Lightning Source LLC
Chambersburg PA
CBHW041713210326
41598CB00007B/641